ARCHIBALD LAMPMAN

CANADIAN POET OF NATURE

BY
CARL Y. CONNOR
B.A. (Toronto), A.M. (Harvard), Ph.D. (Columbia),
Formerly Fellow and Instructor in Columbia University.
Professor of English, Sweet Briar College, Virginia.

FOREWORD BY
RAY PALMER BAKER
M.A., Ph.D.

Borealis Press Limited
Ottawa, Canada,
1977

ISBN 0 919 594 75-1

Published with the assistance of the
Ontario Arts Council

The Borealis Press Limited
9 Ashburn Drive
Ottawa, Canada. K2E 6N4

Printed and Bound in Canada

Second Edition

PREFACE

◇

It is difficult to express in brief space sufficient gratitude to the many people who have helped in the preparation of this book on Archibald Lampman. Nothing could better attest the high regard in which his memory is held than their cordiality in assisting to recall and record the facts of his life and work.

To his relatives, Dr. E. and Mrs. Voorhis, Mrs. F. M. S. Jenkins, Mr. and Mrs. Loftis McInnes and Mrs. Catharine Playter Armstrong, I am greatly indebted, especially to Dr. Voorhis for Chapters One and Thirteen, and also to Dr. D. C. Scott, Lampman's literary executor, to Mr. J. A. Ritchie, his college friend, to Mr. W. J. Sykes, of the Ottawa Public Library, and to Dr. Tait McKenzie of the University of Pennsylvania.

In Toronto, Rev. H. O. Tremayne and Rev. G. H. Broughall, as well as Mr. M. O. Hammond of the "Globe" and the librarians and staffs of the Reference and Trinity College Libraries, were very helpful.

Dr. Ray Palmer Baker of the Rensselaer Polytechnic Institute, Dr. Gerhard Lomer, Librarian of McGill University, and Professors A. H. Thornike and R. L. Rusk of Columbia University were of great assistance as was Professor W. P. Trent of Columbia under whose invaluable direction the work was carried on.

To these and many others I extend my sincerest thanks for material, encouragement and guidance.

CARL Y. CONNOR.

SPRINGFIELD,
Ontario.

Archibald Lampman
1861 - 1899

ARCHIBALD LAMPMAN

Canadian Poet of Nature

CONTENTS

The frontispiece is from a drawing by A. Dickson Patterson, R.C.A., based on an unpublished photograph in the possession of Lorne Pierce, F.R.S.C., LL.D.

The medallion of Archibald Lampman reproduced on the Jacket is from a plaque in Trinity College School by R. Tait McKenzie, M.D., LL.D.

FOREWORD

MOST estimates of Archibald Lampman have been affected by the tendency to consider him not as he was but as he might have been. One merit of this study by Dr. Connor is its undeviating realism. He has shown that the position attained by the author of "Among the Millet" is due to his integration with the life of which he was a part. "I have been endeavouring," wrote Lampman, "to think up some plan for a strictly Canadian poem, local in its incident and spirit, but cosmopolitan in form and manner"; and if his poetry is not national, it is at least richly and finely provincial. More accurately and more delicately than any other writer of his day, he has reproduced the atmosphere of Old Ontario: the reverberating fields of April; the powdered roads of August with the shimmer of heat on the horizon; the flaming landscapes of October, and the glittering hills of January under the star-lit sky. Nor has any writer of his day portrayed more sympathetically and more subtly the temper of his generation,—a generation that was never impassioned and that was never great but that was, at its best, unobtrusively responsive to the harmonies and discords of existence. It is this immediacy that gives to the work of Lampman whatever universality it possesses.

Because of his insistence upon this point of view, Dr Connor's volume is of a significant contribution. Lampman's contemporaries, Mr. Roberts and Mr. Carman, have been treated by Professor Cappon and Professor Shepard; but their studies—the studies of a Scot and an

American—are primarily essays in æsthetics, written largely *in vacuo*. They seldom touch the background—still unknown in the world of letters—from which the literature of the Dominion has emerged. Dr. Connor's monograph, on the other hand, is founded on the knowledge that springs from experience and understanding as well as from interest and scholarship. Every chapter is reminiscent of the years which he has spent beside the Great Lakes, on the Prairies, or among the mountains of British Columbia. Nevertheless, although he has written as a Canadian, familiar with the cultural development of his native land, he has also written as a student whose taste has been formed in the schools and universities of Europe and the United States. His judgments are, therefore, characterized by a sense of proportion that is often lacking in contemporary criticism. As a man and a writer, Lampman appears not as a seer and a master, but as a clerk and a craftsman who, in his happiest moments, is not unworthy of this memorial.

RAY PALMER BAKER

Department of Arts, Science and Business Administration,
Rensselaer Polytechnic Institute,
Troy, New York.

TO MY PARENTS

WITH AFFECTION

INTRODUCTION

HE quiet, penetrating power of genius never ceases to astonish, and Emerson's dictum that the world will wear a pathway to the threshold of the obscure but truly great, continues to be true. In the 1800's and '90's Ontario was isolated enough, but it produced a quiet clerk in the Civil Service who through the power of his art alone became recognized as Canada's best writer of nature verse, and perhaps the finest poet she had yet inspired. It is true that recognition was deliberate and slow. The first notable critic to discover Lampman was W. D. Howells, who gave him access to the American magazines. In time his poetry was reviewed in France, in Germany, and in England, where the London *Spectator* ranked it with Longfellow's. It was remarked upon in distant Honolulu and by Robert Louis Stevenson crossing the Pacific. To the Canadian people it has always seemed peculiarly national and praiseworthy and, though never very popular, it has continued to be read by successive generations of Canadians and to win the appreciation of the discriminating in various lands. The reason is not far to seek. It is because Archibald Lampman was a writer whose appeal was twofold, both national and universal.

By various tokens he was national. Practically all his short life was lived in Ontario. His forbears were typical United Empire Loyalists, handing on a tradition of devotion to Canada and the Empire. His formative years were spent in one of the most beautiful lake districts in Ontario. In school and college his training was typically Canadian, and his later years in the Dominion capital were productive of poetry essentially descriptive of the Canadian scene. But, in addition to this, his work took on a wider aspect. His philosophy of life knew no national bounds. His kinship was with a nature not merely Canadian. His craftsmanship raised his verse into the unprovincial realms of art.

Into the making of a poet many factors enter, and to judge him justly it is necessary to go back several generations. The legacy of Lampman's ancestors seems to have been twofold, of the body and of the mind, for in him met the two strains of farmer and scholar. His parents had an important part in his mental and emotional development. From his mother came, in the main, his æstheticism, from his father, his mind. In addition, there was in youth the influence of exceptionally beautiful natural surroundings, the encouraging interest of older people, and the inspiration from his teachers, his classmates and his books. With college days came wider interests and new aims. Finally he settled down in a Government office to devote his leisure to Nature, to a few friends, and to the perfecting of his Art.

The most tangible result of Lampman's life is the poetry which he has left. That will be saved or discarded as posterity sees fit. Perhaps it is as imperishable as the sky and fields of which he wrote. Perhaps it will become merely an interesting prelude to the greater Canadian poetry of the future. But his personal influence also remains in the lives of the people with whom he came in contact, few though they were in comparison to his readers. To them his personality was elusive but powerful. His varying moods of sweetness, whimsicality, vigour and melancholy live only in their memories and cannot fully be recaptured. By instinct or design little of this was written into his verse. There are thus, the two Lampmans, the poet and the man. Yet they are complementary rather than contradictory. To know both is to understand and appreciate him as he really was.

CHAPTER I.

ANCESTRY.

N a day in May, in the year 1860 in Trinity Church, Morpeth, Ontario, Archibald Lampman, the rector of the church, was married to Susanna Charlotte, daughter of David Henry Gesner, the veritable *seigneur* of the district. These were the father and mother of Archibald Lampman, the poet, who was born in the rectory at Morpeth on the morning of Sunday, November 17th, 1861.

Both Lampmans and Gesners were of United Empire Loyalist stock and their ancestors had endured pioneer hardships in emigrating, first to America from Holland and Hanover, and later to Canada during the American Revolution. But with that their similarity ceased, for the Gesners of Swiss origin were short and dark, men of literary culture, naturalists, classical scholars, professors of mathematics and theologians; while the Lampmans were hard-headed Hanoverian Germans; fine types of manhood and typical pioneers in their fondness for the woods and farms. This intimacy with nature the poet would seem to have inherited from them, but he showed his Gesner ancestry in his short stature, oval face and brown hair, in his keen judgment of literature and men, in his fondness for the classics, and in the thoughtful, studious quality of his mind.

Frederick Lampman, the great-great grandfather of the poet, stands out, a pathetic and heroic figure in the early records of the times. Born in Hanover in 1719, he had emigrated to America and settled in New Jersey, where he lived for over thirty years till, with the outbreak of the American Revolution, his loyalist principles forced him at the age of sixty-five to seek a new home in Canada. His son, Peter, also experienced the hardships of the Revolution, first in his escape into Canada, during which he had to hide in trees and hay-stacks from the Americans, and later when he returned to New York for his English wife, who with their small children travelled on horseback while her husband trudged by her side. When he came to die in 1834 at the age of 85, he had the satisfaction of seeing his original holdings on which he had chopped down trees for his log house, become a productive fruit-farm. This property between Thorold and St. Catharines, which he had named "Mountain Point," was inherited by the third of his ten children, Peter, who married Agnes McNeal, daughter of Archibald McNeal a Scottish settler from Baltimore. They also had ten children and the third son, Archibald, born in 1822, was the father of the poet. He was educated at Upper Canada College, Toronto, graduated from Trinity College in 1857, and soon after being ordained into the Ministry of the Church of England went to Morpeth as rector of Trinity Church. It was there that he met his future wife, Susanna Gesner.

Like the Lampmans, the Gesners were Loyalist emigrants from the United States, but they were of a prouder spirit and more cultured background. Their previous history had been illustrious ever since a branch of the family had moved from Switzerland into Germany in the fifteenth century.

On June 10th, 1710, the ship *Lyon*, which arrived in the port of New York, still a mere village, though no longer under control of the Netherlands, numbered among its passengers John Hendrick Gesner, the poet's great-great grandfather. He settled at Tappan, about thirty miles north of New York, and became owner of a farm and grist-mill to which his son, similarly named, succeeded him. This son became the father of twin boys, Henry and Abraham. When eighteen years of age the twins enlisted in the loyalist forces, were present at the storming of Fort Montgomery and did garrison duty at Halifax, Nova Scotia, where they later received land grants and were among the first to develop large fruit farms in the Cornwallis and Annapolis valleys.

Henry, now called "Colonel," was a man with a reputation for family pride, autocracy and reserve. Of his twelve children, one, Abraham, born in Cornwallis in 1797, seemed to show some of the scientific talent of his continental ancestors. After studying medicine in England, he returned to practice at Parrsboro, N.S., where he also collected geological specimens, and in 1836 published *Remarks on the Geology and Mineralogy of Nova Scotia*, a work which not only resulted in his appointment two years later as Provincial Geologist of New Brunswick, but also gained for him the unofficial title of "Father of Canadian Geology."

His brother David, four years his senior, also studied medicine and taught school in Montreal; but, attracted by a love of adventure and a fondness for the country, journeyed with a company of others in the year 1825 to Port Talbot, on the north shore of Lake Erie. Here Colonel Talbot, a retired English army officer and one of the most picturesque figures in colonial settlement, had been granted 100,000 acres of land on condition that he would place a settler on every 200 acres. David Gesner's farm, seven miles along the Talbot Road from Morpeth, was almost solid bush, and there he experienced all the privations of pioneer life, without comforts and cut off from family and friends. First he felled enough timber for a log house and then began to clear the land, mindful of his father's fruitful farm at Cornwallis. For two years he lived alone, and by the end of that time was in a position to offer a home, such as it was, to Sarah Stewart, whose Scotch father had emigrated from Tyrone County, Ireland, and whose mother was of a Knickerbocker family named Culver. In brown hair and eyes, and in gentleness of disposition, she was later said to be resembled by her grandson, the poet. In contrast, her husband was a stern man whose experiences and inherited force of character combined to make him an outstanding figure in the community, and the Government, seeing in him a loyalist who might prove valuable in case of American invasion or Canadian disaffection, made him Crown Commissioner and later Justice of the Peace and King's Councillor. His word was law throughout the district, and his neighbors are said to have consulted him on all important undertakings. Like his father, he was very proud-spirited, difficult of approach, and intolerant of opposition. This attitude he also maintained toward his family, whose careers he no doubt hampered. Of his eight children only two married; the eldest son, John, and Susannah Charlotte, the poet's mother. Fortunately she inherited little of her father's autocracy of temper, but her determined disposition and her gift for music, both powerful factors in forming the characters of her children, came from him, and the practical thrift inherited from her Scotch mother stood her in good stead later, under conditions when an equally ambitious but less sagacious woman must have failed.

The history of the Lampman and Gesner families is the old romantic story of Europeans adapting themselves to New World conditions; of families forced to leave one country for another through the strength of their convictions. The Gesners, descendants of Swiss scholars, became New York State millers; military fruit-farmers and early

Nova Scotia scientists; Ontario pioneers. The Lampmans, with less brilliance but even greater hardihood, after clearing farms for themselves in the Canadian bush, in time gave rise to college-trained ministers of the Church of England. Together they were typical of the two classes of settlers which came to Canada after the American Revolutionary War; the cultured and the comparatively uneducated, the brain and the brawn. In general, Maritime Canada claimed the former, for some of the best legal and clerical minds of New England were represented among the emigrants to the Canadian sea-board. To Upper Canada, on the other hand, went less-cultured people like the Lampmans whose contributions to Canadian thought and literature came at a later date. The laws and workings of heredity are still mysterious and unformulated; but it is not impossible to see these two strains mingling and playing their part in the slow creation of a Canadian poet, who was not only a Lampman in thoroughness of thought and expression and fondness for life in the open, but also a Gesner in sensitivity, in culture and in distinction of mind.

CHAPTER II.

EARLY LIFE.

HEN in 1861 Lampman was born in Morpeth, the village was at the height of its prosperity. Beginning as a halting place at the top of a hill difficult for travellers westward on the Talbot Road, it had ceased to flourish only when the construction of the Canada Southern Railway diverted traffic farther north. Three or four grist mills were built along the creek which ran at the foot of the steep hill, and nearby was the port of Antrim on Lake Erie, the scene of great activity on shipping days, when the farmer's wagons waited in long lines to unload their grain.

About a mile and a half east of Morpeth in Howard Township stood Trinity Church, built in 1844-45, partially through the generosity of Colonel Talbot's relative, Lord Morpeth, whose name was given to the parish and village. Of this church, the poet's father was rector. It had the distinction of being located on the highest point in the county of Kent, and from it one could get a wide view of Lake Erie and the surrounding country. The rectory was situated about a quarter of a mile south of the village, between the Tabolt Road and Lake Erie. This small, plain, brick house, guiltless of "architecture" and without verandah or porch, was the poet's birthplace.

Lampman's infancy was not remarkable from a domestic viewpoint. He showed no signs of "lisping in number," nor any early predisposition to any but the usual catastrophes and diseases of normal childhood. But historically his youth was surrounded by wars and rumors of war.

With the outbreak of the American Civil War in April, 1861, there had been talk of annexation of Canada and English intervention. Canadian pioneer settlers, like the poet's grandfather, to whom the War of 1812 was a vivid recollection, were naturally much concerned over the defence of their very vulnerable border, and consequently there was soon a mustering of volunteers and an assembling of ancient weapons. But in time the panic abated, though it was revived five years later when a party of Irish-Americans, the Fenians, actually did cross into Canada.

In the year 1866, when Archie Lampman was five years old, his father was appointed rector of the Anglican Church at Perrytown, a village in the county of Durham nine miles from Port Hope, and more than two hundred miles from Morpeth, their first home. It was with some reluctance that they left the Morpeth district, for there Mrs. Lampman had been born, educated, and married; there Mr. Lampman had suffered and enjoyed most of the experiences which come to a minister fresh from college, and there Archie and his younger sister Sarah Isabelle had been born.

Perrytown, in quite another part of Ontario, was a quiet little inland village situated in a sparsely settled part of the country, while Morpeth, though a village also, was almost on the shores of Lake Erie and lay on the main line of travel between eastern and western Ontario. The Lampmans were just beginning to adjust themselves to new conditions when, within a year, an opportunity was given Mr. Lampman to become rector of the church at Gore's Landing, on Rice Lake, and he accepted it with alacrity.

Gore's Landing has had an interesting history ever since the days when the Indians used to gather there for the fish and game which fed on the wild rice growing so abundantly along its shores. It lay along a route taken by the first English settlers who, beginning at Montreal and following the St. Lawrence river and Lake Ontario, turned inland at Cobourg to Rice Lake, the first of a series of waterways leading many miles further on. The surrounding country was rolling, fertile and richly wooded, and the picturesque scenery, together with the prospect of abundant game, appealed to Englishmen in search of new homes. The district, therefore, was settled early by emigrants from the old land.

To move from Perrytown in its uninteresting surroundings to the more beautiful and romantic scenery of Rice Lake was a pleasant prospect for all the Lampman family. Even Archie, aged six, and his three-year-old sister were aware of new interests which might be provided by life beside a real lake on which one could sail in boats and perhaps be permitted to catch fish. Annie Margaret, aged one, might be regarded as still too young to show very much interest in the scenic surroundings of her new home. The only difficulty arose from the fact that in Gore's Landing houses were at a premium. It was not a large place, the population being around five hundred, but it was most attractively situated on the sloping side of one of the wooded hills which rise from the western end of the lake. There was a main street which followed the shore line, a few stores, a hotel, wharves, boathouses, pleasant little cottages, a half-dozen more pretentious houses, and at the top of the hill, among the trees, the little rough-cast church of which Mr. Lampman was to be rector. From there you could look out over the still water, with its reed-lined banks, to the islands farther down in the centre of the lake. Sometimes they were double islands, so perfectly was their foliage reflected in the clear water; sometimes they were wind-blown tufts of trees among tossing waves; in early morning they were faint blue shapes floating in rosy mist, and beneath the moon they lay dark and tranquil on a polished mirror sown with stars. Such surroundings are strangely potent, even for a boy aged six.

But the shortage of houses was a real difficulty, for the only vacant building was an old stone tavern which stood on the main street of the town. Here, indeed, was a perplexing situation for a new rector. Perhaps, after due reflection, he recollected that poets have lodged in garrets and Bunyan had lived in jail. At any rate there was nothing to do but accept the tavern and the inevitable, and presently he and his family were in the anomalous and even amusing situation of occupying quarters but recently vacated by a vendor of spirituous liquors.

The first months of Gore's Landing were given over to settling, for it is not an easy task to transform a tavern into a rectory, and not even after the placing of ministerial furniture was the metamorphosis quite complete; nor would it be surprising if the mind of some male parishioner in audience with his pastor in what was once the bar strayed, at times, to other days and other ways.

Life for the Lampmans was very busy, especially for Mrs. Lampman, for not only did she have the three children to look after and housekeeping to attend to, but she was very ambitious for her husband's success in the new parish. She played the organ at services in the little church, did a good deal of parochial visiting, and was given over heart and soul to the education and well-being of the children.

In due time Archie was sent to school and presently also Sarah Isabelle, who trotted along proudly at his side, much envied by the younger Annie Margaret. There was, too, a younger sister, Caroline Stewart, born in 1868, thus making a family of four.

Then something almost tragic happened, for Archie suddenly fell seriously ill of rheumatic fever. He had always been fairly vigorous, but the air of Rice Lake was damp and, in addition, the old tavern with its leaky roof rattling windows and mouldy plaster walls, was really barely habitable. When, after weeks of illness, the crisis had passed, it was found that the fever had left its effects in that weakness of the heart which was ultimately to cause his death, and more pathetic still, small pieces of bone had come out of his ankle during the illness, and it seemed that perhaps the little boy would be lame for the rest of his life. Expert medical advice was not to be had in the village, and so, when he was well enough, his mother took him to a doctor in St. Catharines. When she returned she was very sad, for the doctor had advised amputation. It seemed a rigorous measure, and beside there was really no money for an operation. In desperation she took him to another physician, Dr. Dewar of Port Hope.

"Amputation?" said Dr. Dewar, "By no means, my good woman, by no means. Give the boy fresh air, good food, plenty of exercise and—cod liver oil!"

Everyone was pleased, except Archie. He did not like cod liver oil. In fact he had to be bribed to take it. Finally, after weeks of payment, a long-awaited sum was reached. He had been looking forward to that moment with great excitement. In one grand, deliberate, single extravagance he spent it, for he purchased a "Universal History of the World."

Another favorite book of his was Abbot's "History of Napoleon," which he read in his father's library. From that moment Napoleon became his supreme hero. The margins of his school books were adorned with sketches of the European despot in all sorts of poses, and so far did he carry his hero worship that he had more than one spirited argument with his father, who entertained much less cordial views of Mr. Abbott and his illustrious subject.

It was at about this time that Archie came under the

influence of one of the most famous of early Canadian educators, Mr. F. W. Barron, M.A. of Cambridge, and one time principal of Upper Canada College, Toronto. Formerly he had had his school in a bay-windowed building which jutted out into the Cobourg King Street. But when it was burned down he decided to remove to Rice Lake, where greater isolation and unrivalled natural surroundings would contribute to the control and development of his pupils. There were a score or more of these, from eight to twenty years of age, coming from eastern Canada and the United States. Most of them were being prepared for Upper Canada College or the Universities, and some had been especially sent for training under the rigorous rule of a teacher who had a widespread reputation for discipline of an order sometimes associated with the British militia. Each morning he would appear before his pupils like a figure out of the pages of Charles Dickens. He was English pedagogy personified, and he bore before him on a red cushion the symbols of his office—the Bible and the rod. Yet, in spite of this, Mr. Barron was not an ogre. Sometimes on a particularly fine afternoon he would say, "Well, boys, what do you say to a sail on the lake? Some other time we will make up for what we lose today." To teach boys to sail a boat properly was one of Mr. Barron's chief delights. The boys swam in summer, and on winter afternoons and nights you could hear their shouts as they played hockey or followed the leader on their skates. Mr. Barron was most thorough and efficient as a teacher, but though his pupils were hard worked and well disciplined they had a good time. Most of them lived at his house, a low, rambling building, smothered in vines and adjoining the church. It was presided over by Mrs. Barron, as typical an Engish housewife as her husband was a schoolmaster. Altogether it was a distinct advantage to Gore's Landing to have Mr. Barron and his boys in its midst.

To one of them it was an untold benefit, for it put him in touch at an early age with the best traditions of English education, it encouraged the reading already begun in his father's library, and it was the beginning of his life-long study of the classics. In a short time Archie Lampman had become Mr. Barron's prize pupil.

From the unsuitable, if picturesque, old tavern, the Lampmans next moved to a capacious brick rectory across the bay from the church. It was a comfortable old house less than a hundred yards from the lake shore. At one corner bloomed a great yellow rose bush, and in the centre of the garden a large syringa. At one end was a vegetable garden and at the other, Mrs. Lampman's, all flowers. In between lay the children's gardens, one for each, which they cultivated not without rivalry.

Naturally, during the summer they spent much of their time in or on the water. All of them were taught early to swim, Archie becoming one of the best swimmers in the school. Rice Lake was famous for its *muskalonge* and black bass, and Archie's luck as a fisherman was proverbial in the family. Often, too, they had picnics down the shore or on one of the islands. Occasionally the parents would spend the evening with friends in town, and then there would be great fun in the old house: pillow fights, hide-and-go-seek in the upper rooms and closets, and even descent to the lower floor by way of the banisters.

The one luxury which the rectory possessed was the piano, which had caused many a sacrifice before its purchase was possible. All the children were taught by their mother to play, and the second sister was destined to study in Germany and become a leader in the musical circles in the city in which she lived. By the time Archie was ten he could play simple pianoforte music quite well. For the song "Bonnie Dundee" he conceived as great a passion as he had had for the character of Napoleon Bonaparte, and he frequently gave spirited renditions of this piece to his own accompaniment. Two years later a change had taken place. He no longer practised, and deemed piano-playing fit only for girls. Yet in reality music always meant much to him. In his college days he became especially fond of martial songs and poetry. Of his later poems which definitely have music for their theme (1) one, "The Child's Music Lesson," seems to recall his own efforts at the old piano, and to set him wishing for it, and the rectory garden and the return of those happy, distant days.

In the Rice Lake society of those times there was much pleasant visiting. The Atwoods, Sorbys, Barrons, and Captain Thompsons were among the chief families. Sometimes Archie would be taken by his parents to call. He had a fancy for clocks, and no visit was complete unless he had been shown the family time-piece. He was universally a favorite, especially with people much older than himself, for already there were signs of that indefinable charm which was to make all who knew him in later years feel that he was really a man apart, one to whom commonplaces of this life are of secondary concern, whose real life is of the spirit.

The most famous of these grown friends were Mrs. Moodie and Mrs. Traill, so noteworthy in early Canadian

---

(1) "The Organist." An organist whose playing has attracted a young girl, falls in love with her, but she learns to love another, and he is found dead at his keyboard.

"The Child's Music Lesson." Probably written at the Nicholas Street cottage, Ottawa. Seated in the garden, the poet hears from the house a child's unsuccessful attempt to play its lesson, and he recalls his own childhood.

"Music." Inspired by his sister Annie (Mrs. Jenkins), whose music brought "Keen glimpses of life's splendour, dashing gleams of what we would, and what we cannot be."

"The Violinist." A blind fiddler in a Dresden street is befriended by a musician who plays so marvelously on the old violin that the listeners fill the beggar's hat with money. It is learned later that the musician was Spohr.

"Music" and "The Piano." Two sonnets describing the effect of music in transferring the listener into an almost clairvoyant state in which he sees with undimmed eyes the pageant of the Past and the Future.

literature as examples of an old-world culture taking root in and fructifying a new. The sisters, born in England, were christened Susanna and Catharine Parr Strickland. Their parents were people of wealth and culture; their sisters, Agnes and Elizabeth, were joint authors of a series of "Lives of the Queens of England," and they themselves had written children's stories and verse before 1832 when they emigrated to Canada, the wives of two soldier-pioneers.

In the "Backwoods of Canada," which was published in London in 1836 and widely read, especially by prospective emigrants, Mrs. Traill gave a graphic description of her adventures, and though she did not minimize the hardships, the book was brightened by the gentle optimism which was so characteristic of her nature, and which endeared her to her fellow-travellers, her settler neighbors, and many years later to young Archie Lampman, then a school-boy playing about the shores of Rice Lake. In spite of primitive conditions, little money, few comforts, and the cares of a family of nine, Mrs. Traill not only wrote novels of Canadian backwoods life but continued her study of botany and the collections of specimens which resulted, in 1884, in the publication of "Studies of Plant Life in Canada," illustrated by her niece, Mrs. Chamberlin, a book which, considering the circumstances under which it was written, is, in accuracy and care, a remarkable achievement.

Mrs. Moodie's "Roughing it in the Bush," published in London in 1852, is the book by which she is best known though she also wrote novels, and, with her husband, published the "Victoria Magazine" in Belleville for a year in 1847, an unsuccessful venture which attested, however, a seriousness which like that of other Canadians such as John Gibson and John Lovell, sponsors of the "Literary Garland," was typical of the time. Their concern in endeavouring to raise the standards of thought and reading seems very genuine. Mrs. Moodie and Mrs. Traill entered whole-heartedly into the life of the colony, and their advantages of talent and training seemed only to put upon them a willing obligation to contribute to its progress.

It was Mrs. Traill whom the Lampmans knew best. The children remembered her as a kind old lady with beautiful white hair worn in cork-screw curls under an immaculate white-frilled, long-stringed cap. The vicissitudes of her life and the mingling with people less fortunate in birth, education and native gifts, had not affected her gentility. The children loved to listen to her conversation; it was all so interesting and understandable and yet she had "such a literary style of speaking."

Naturally she was attracted to Archie, who was also one of Mr. Barron's favorites. In a short piece called "The Cranberry Marsh," she wrote:

"Just fancy a young field naturalist returning from an exploring tour in the cranberry marsh. He is hot and tired, a good deal fly-bitten, delapitated in dress and appearance, somewhat the worse for wear, but with looks that tell of unexpected good fortune.

Having hastily satisfied his hunger and thirst at the camp, he unstraps his japanned case, his face beaming with triumphant smiles, and proceeds to exhibit his wonderful finds in the shape of rare beetles of metallic hues, green, red, scarlet, blue, and sulphur-colored; dragon flies large and small, bronze, blue, red, or metallic green; silvery moths with dappled wings or elegant blue ones with brilliant eyes.

"From a pill-box which he carries carefully in his vest-pocket he takes a tiny land tortoise, no bigger than a black beetle, that he found basking in the sand near a creek and only just hatched from its warm shady nest.

"And then he will be off next morning at sunrise to the big peat moss which he has not yet had leisure to explore." (1)

There is no evidence that the young naturalist was Archie Lampman, but the woman who wrote these paragraphs may have had considerable influence on a poet who always took with him a botanist's equipment on his camping trips, and one of the chief merits of whose verse is the amazing skill and accuracy with which he records the sights and sounds and colours of the out-of-doors.

To estimate the effect of the Rice Lake period on the unfolding mind of Canada's nature poet is a difficult matter, and its results must necessarily be problematical. The years from six to thirteen are among the most impressionable in any boy's life. For Archie Lampman they were especially so. Already he had come to know what pain was and the inconvenience of crutches. In his home for all its frugality, he was surrounded with a wealth of affection from his studious father, his energetic, ambitious mother, and his devoted sisters. He had for his schoolmaster a man skilled in the training of boys, who became not only an inspiration but a friend. To have known the kindly, cultivated Mrs. Traill, whose keen mind was so alert to the people and things about her, must in itself have been a stimulus. He had at his disposal at least two libraries, his father's and Mr. Barron's, and it is plain that he made use of them and started one of his own. More than all, by a happy accident, he grew up in one of the most lovely districts in Ontario, less rugged but otherwise comparable in beauty and charm to the English lakes of William Wordsworth. It is true that he left not one poem which can definitely be said to have Rice Lake as its source of inspiration, but the following description written

---

(1) "Pearls and Pebbles, or Notes of an Old Naturalist," *by* Catharine Parr Traill, Toronto, 1895.

when he was a man of thirty shows that its influence was powerful, and that its scenes were not forgotten:

"I remember a lake with a long mid-winter road running across its frozen surface marked with young cedars fading into the distance, an infinite dotted line, and I remember the jingling teams that would come by this track on the crystal Christmas mornings, bound for the little rough-cast church on the hilltop above the landing. I remember the rough-voiced farmers, bearded white with hoar frost, and the cheerful ruddy-faced women, and the good words they had, and the presents they always brought with them for the parson—a turkey, a goose, a side of pork, a couple of bags of oats, some pairs of knitted socks and many another thing. I remember how the lake roared under the moonlit Christmas night as if all the northern genii were gathered like Merlin's chained fiends at Caermarden under that gleaming band of ice, and all night long the imprisoned waters groaned and struggled, now with reports as of pistols and now with a thunder as of a hundred cannon. I remember the yearly expedition into the silent woods, when some luckless young pine, delicately tufted or beautifully pointed cedar was cut and pruned for the Christmas tree. Every Canadian who has spent a boyhood in the country where the northern lakes are, remembers these things and many more at Christmas; his heart warms to the like dreamers about him; he thinks well of his country and the people who have made it; and the old words repeat themselves upon his tongue with an especial tenderness, 'Peace on earth and good-will to men.'"

CHAPTER III.

BOYHOOD.

THE Cobourg of the 1870's, when the Lampmans moved into it from Rice Lake, was a pleasant town for the Ontario of those days. Situated on Lake Ontario, it had already begun to attract summer visitors, and behind it was the rich, rolling farming district of Northumberland County. It had been founded early in the history of the province, for it lay in the path of the pioneers and later of the Loyalists, who landed less than a hundred miles east along the coast. Many of the original settlers and their descendants were living there and maintained in comfortable homes and grounds the manners and social graces of their ancestors. It was, moreover, the seat of Victoria University, founded there by the Methodist Church, as Upper Canada Academy in 1836 and Victoria College in 1841. To it came young men from all over the province to take courses in arts or theology. Thus Cobourg was a town beautiful in surroundings and not without an atmosphere of aristocracy and learning.

On King Street East, facing the Lake and surrounded with fine trees, stood the stone church of St. Peter's. The Reverend Walter Stennet, a son-in-law of Bishop A. N. Bethune, was rector, and to it Mr. Lampman came as curate in 1874. Across the street, a block or two nearer the centre of the town, stood a terrace of red brick houses, and into one of these, No. 37, the Lampmans moved. It was a well-built house of three stories and an attic, tall and narrow. From the street one entered directly through a little enclosed porch into a long hall. On the left was a dignified parlor with a high ceiling and two large-paned windows, which looked out on the street. There you could see the butcher's cart going by in the morning or a trio of students from Victoria hurrying down town, their tongues chattering and their gowns flying in the breeze. Behind the parlor and the hall, which made a sharp left turn toward the staircase leading to the upper floors, was the living room. It was a square room, large enough for a whole family to draw round the table in the centre or to sit in front of the plain old fireplace. From its windows, when the leaves were off the trees, one might catch a glimpse of Lake Ontario, and in summer a door opened on a small back lawn and garden.

The salary of the curate of St. Peter's was not very large in those days, and so presently Mr. and Mrs. Lampman, who were by nature educators, opened a school in the King Street house. On the floor above the living room was a bedroom of similar proportions, and this soon became a schoolroom for a dozen children of the town whose parents did not wish them to attend a public school. Over this Mrs. Lampman presided, while her husband in the parlor instructed a group of youths in mathematics and the classics.

Archie's sisters were educated at home, but he entered the Cobourg Collegiate Institute at the age of thirteen. This institution had grown years before out of a union of the town Grammar School and the College Preparatory Department. By this means students insufficiently prepared for college in some subjects could come to Cobourg and take classes at both College and Collegiate. It had, therefore, a somewhat higher standard through its association with Victoria.

In the morning the whole school assembled for hymns, Bible reading and prayers, after which the girls were conducted to special classrooms, or modestly occupied the front benches in mixed classes, in those early days of co-education.

From September to December, Archie attended the preparatory class, after which he passed into the Collegiate Institute proper. The report of the latter institution for the half year ending June, 1876, which he brought home to his ambitious parents, was very gratifying and read as follows: "Latin Grammar—1. A. Lampman. Neatness in written work—2. A. Lampman. Algebra—2. A. Lampman and J. Watt, equal. History of Greece and Rome—1. A. Lampman." He seems not to have availed himself of such subjects as Anabasis, Natural Philosophy, Analysis of English Classics, Reading and Elocution, etc. Nor did he take much part in the spelling matches which were then so popular that they even escaped the bounds of school and were held amid vast excitementin Pomeroy's Hall. The neatness in written work is not surprising, for throughout his life he could, when he took pains, write a beautiful, clear, flowing hand. This writing was a curiously transmitted family characteristic, for there is a marked similarity in the hand-writing of the poet, one of his sisters and his daughter. But the school report of 1876 must not be taken to mean that Archie was a scholastic prodigy, and it is good to know that one of his schoolmates' most vivid recollections of him is of a boy who was not above pushing the other boys off their bench in class

Mrs. Lampman was always determined that the children should have every opportunity for development. For instance, she encouraged some of her musical friends to come and play, that the family might become acquainted with the best in music. These musicales were unforgettable. At the piano in the stately parlor would sit an equally stately player performing a sonata with seriousness and solemnity. The children behaved with a decorum suited to the occasion, but it would not be at all surprising if the music seemed a little heavy; and long after, Archie, who never liked Brahms, was heard to voice a temporary grotesque mood in the following impromptu composition:

> "On hearing a sonata by Brahms
> You should straightway get down on your hams
> And utter ten thousand damns
> Long-drawn in the manner of psalms."

Yet, in spite of this seeming failure, Mrs. Lampman's musical methods were seen later to be more than justified.

The year which Archie spent at Cobourg was one of transition. He had had to leave the pleasant freedom of life in the old rectory by Rice Lake, and had come to live in a tall house in the main street of the town. No doubt he missed the old associations, though from the room at the top of the house where long after his death one could read the name "A. Lampman" scrawled in pencil on the inside of the closet door, he could look out over Lake Ontario, so brilliantly blue in summer days, so bleak and cold in winter. He was keeping up a good record at school, but this seemed to concern him little. His reading was mostly in books of history and travel. Of poetry there was as yet no sign.

In September, 1876, at the age of fifteen, Archie entered Trinity College School, Port Hope. First founded in Weston by the Rev. W. A. Johnson, it had been moved in 1865 under the Rev. C. H. Badgley's headmastership to Port Hope. There a spacious old farmhouse, the Ward homestead, had been rented and classrooms engaged in the Registry office in the town half a mile away. But after two years Mr. Badgley, a remarkable teacher and disciplinarian, resigned and was succeeded by the Rev. C. J. S. Bethune, son of the Bishop of Toronto, under whom for more than twenty years the school increased in prosperity and influence. It was due to Mr. Bethune and Mr. John Cartwright that Archie was enabled to spend the next two years at the principal Anglican boys' school of the province.

The confidence placed in him was fully justified, for he was probably one of the most studious boys at the school. Slight and frail, though not delicate, he seemed always to be reading or studying. The little boys in his dormitory could remember being half awakened by Lampman coming up to bed after studying to an hour which seemed very late to them. For mathematics he had no taste, but he liked literature and the classics. During one vacation he read the Odyssey in the original, not as a task but for pleasure, though it must have been fairly difficult. Naturally he took many prizes, and in his second year was Head Boy and Prefect of the school. There were twelve prefects of whom he was head, and their duties were to attend to the discipline of the boys after school, maintain order in the corridors, take turns supervising the junior study, and hold roll-call every morning and afternoon. As prefect of Room No. 10, later known as the Military Room, he was liked but never feared. No boy would ever be intimidated by him, and yet no boy with the least sense of kindliness would ever have antagonized him. Though not active in sport, he took a keen interest in cricket, football and hockey, was an excellent skater and the second best swimmer in the school. He was a favorite with the masters, and on Speech Day he was carried with much jubilation through the grounds and school on the shoulders of the boys he had beaten in examinations. Yet he remained quiet and unspoiled, and sometimes he would make friends with the most apparently uncongenial boys. Once, on one of his week-end visits to Cobourg, he took home with him a boy so thoroughly boyish that his chief delight was a vigorous rendition of the song which relates what will happen "if ye tread on the tail of me coat." To think of that song in a household brought up on the best sonatas!

Perhaps his closest friends in those days were G. H. Broughall and Ned Cayley. Yet Archie though popular was not easy to know intimately, and it was only after a year of acquaintance that these two began to feel themselves his friends. The situation of the school was practically ideal for anyone fond of long walks, and the boys were allowed considerable latitude and not kept strictly within bounds.

South from the school stretched the vast expanse of Lake Ontario; the Hamilton township hills were behind; and eastward, in the distance, was the town of Cobourg. There was none of the secluded, pristine charm of the Rice Lake country, but it was not uninspiring. As a proof of this there is the story that one day the family at 37 King Street, Cobourg, were summoned downstairs by Mr. Lampman shortly after the arrival of the mail from Port Hope. He could be seen in the lower hall, a letter in his hand, obviously much pleased. He read what was in the letter. It was a poem from Archie. Now, Mr. Lampman had been writing poems all his life, very long and very bad poems in the style of Pope, perfectly scanned and full of highly moral and weighty sentiments, but never before had Archie done such a thing. The sisters tried to be pleased, but they regarded it very dubiously. They were not quite sure whether they could stand two poets in successive generations.

All that earlier poetry is now forgotten. Naturally Archie would never mention it at school, but when he left Trinity College School he had a narrow escape from discovery. During the holidays the lockers were being inspected and in Lampman's there was found a crumpled bit of paper. It was unfolded. The writing was just decipherable. It read: "*Lines to the Lake.*"

CHAPTER IV.

COLLEGE DAYS.

'ETAT, c'est moi", said Louis XIV. To Carlyle many an institution was but the elongated shadow of one man. The history of Trinity College is inseparably bound up with the character and life of John Strachan. Born in Aberdeenshire, Scotland, in 1778, he managed, in spite of vicissitudes, to educate himself at the University of St. Andrew's, and there to make friends with Thomas Chalmers, who was later to play an important part in the establishment of the Free Church of Scotland in the early forties of the nineteenth century. When, in 1799, Chalmers declined the headship of a proposed College and University of Upper Canada, here recommended Strachan, who accepted.

On the last day of the year 1799, after a long and uncomfortable journey, Strachan arrived in the colony but found not only that the university of which he was supposed to be head did not exist but that the plans for its establishment had fallen through. As he had no money to return to Scotland, he started a grammar school at Cornwall, where he remained for the next nine years teaching, preaching, and, as he said, "making missionary excursions as a pastime." His executive ability and strong personality made him an outstanding figure wherever he went, and on his removal to York as Rector of the grammar school, he took an active part in the affairs of the community. His diplomacy saved the town from burning by the Americans in the War of 1812. He closely identified himself in politics with the Family Compact party. In 1839 he was appointed by the Crown to be the first Bishop of Toronto.

Yet during all this time he had never lost sight of the original purpose which had brought him to Canada, and in 1827 he had obtained a Royal Charter for the founding of King's College, together with a yearly grant of £1,000, and 500,000 acres of Crown lands. But his work was delayed by the long-drawn-out and bitter quarrel over the Clergy Reserves. In this struggle his uncompromising belief that the Church should be superior in its union with the State led to the founding of Victoria as a Methodist, Queen's as a Presbyterian and finally, Trinity as an Anglican College. The good fighting Bishop was seventy-three years old on the day in 1851 when the corner stone of the new Trinity College was laid. It was to stand not as a mere protest to the divorce of religion from learning but as a testimony of the necessity of religion in the building of perfect all-round manhood. For sixteen years more he lived, raising money when financial depression and the withdrawal of government aid made maintenance difficult and when doctrinal differences within the Corporation itself caused discouragement and discontent. Bishop Strachan was of the stuff of which pioneers are made. He had strong convictions, generous impulses, force and ability, and above all a devotion to the cause of character-building which found expression in Trinity University. And this University, arising as it did from strife and struggle to live up to an ideal, created a tradition among its members which takes on something of the high seriousness of purpose which characterized its illustrious founder.

It was to a college of such traditions that Lampman, now aged seventeen, went as Foundation Scholar in 1879. He had been educated in the Trinity College School atmosphere, corresponding as nearly as might be to the

English public schools. He had proved so brilliant a student at Port Hope that it was confidently expected that his life at Toronto would be one of academic distinction. Indeed, on scholarships would depend the length of his stay at the college. He himself saw that there were at least three courses open to the college student. One was to win scholastic honour, the praise of the masters, and the envy of the other students. He knew something of that. Another was to live the reckless carefree life often attributed to the college man, but circumstances and disposition warned him against such conduct. There remained, however, a middle course, a mingling of study and social enjoyment with a good deal of rambling and desultory reading. Thus far he had lived a somewhat narrow and studious life, and now this third course strongly appealed to him.

It is quite easy to see him, in imagination, on that first day of college, when he comes to Toronto from Cobourg and makes his way out Queen Street to the graceful Tudor buildings standing among the oaks and elms in their thirty or forty acres of grounds. He is a thin youth of medium height, without much animation. As he turns in at the old gates and walks thoughtfully up under the rows of maples, he glances appreciatively at the fine proportions of the buildings, at the fretted beauty of the three decorated stone lantern towers, and at the many pinnacles. He is a raw freshman, neither handsome nor prepossessing, but with a personal charm which is to make itself felt in the college in the days that are ahead.

The original Trinity College had been added to until it might then be said roughly to represent the letter E. Convocation Hall was built north of the main entrance in 1877, and the Chapel in 1883; and the latest additions were students' rooms in the wings.

The freshmen were assigned quarters in the eastern

wing, long known as "The Wilderness." Each man had a room to himself, only a few seniors aspiring to the luxury of studies and double rooms. Most of the rooms had fire-places with an accompanying woodbox. The thick walls were undecorated. The windows were high and narrow; lighting was by gas. The furniture was of the most meagre description—a chair, a bench, a table, a bookcase, a bed and a washstand—all of them bearing obvious evidence of the usage of former occupants. Lampman never bothered to make his room especially attractive. He was much too interested in ideas to be concerned with surroundings.

Naturally he felt a little diffident at first. The corridors and library and chapel were far more impressive than at Port Hope. Most of the boys were new to him. The professors were much less intimate than the masters of a boys' school, but on the other hand there were signs that the sophomores took too much interest in the freshmen. There were tales of newcomers being dragged half-awake through cold, dim corridors to run, blindfolded, a gauntlet of vigorously wielded pillows, or of being "routed," dumped from bed by two grim figures in the dead of night.

During his first term Lampman was a most exemplary student. His attendance at lectures was unfailing. His recitations were unblemished, and he ventured even an occasional deviation from the most approved translations. His interest in football grew, although this was almost obligatory since games were usually preceded by a few Rugby enthusiasts ringing a clamorous dinner-bell through the halls until a general migration to the football field became necessary.

In a short time he became accustomed to college routine. At 7.15 on a winter morning the rising bell at the college would send its unwelcome summons through the long, bleak corridors. Struggling back to consciousness, he would spend the next few minutes wondering whether or not to go to chapel. At the last possible moment he usually decided it would be better to do so, and as a result would arrive dishevelled and half-dressed, to find his fellows gazing yearningly at the empty pews on the senior side, but deprived of the courage to stay away by rumors of reckonings with the Dean or Provost on Saturday mornings. His peace of mind was not improved if the porridge at breakfast proved burned or the steak tough. Then came a half-hour with the newspapers, and before he knew it, another bell was sounding for lectures, to which he again arrived breathless after a search for his usually missing gown. Three hours of Greek verbs, algebra, etc., gave him an excellent appetite for dinner, which was a more cheerful meal, followed by magazine reading and a friendly pipe. The long afternoons were devoted to books or walks or sport, interrupted sometimes by a afternoon call and tea. After supper there came evening chapel fully attended, and finally a night of study, providing he was not interrupted, which was more than likely by some restless prowler whose taste was for talk and food just then, rather than for books.

All the freshmen looked forward to Convocation, for the tradition was that in spite of the dignity of the occasion it was the one opportunity of the year when the boys could do almost as they wished. The custom was supposed to have come from England, and certainly it seemed like harking back to the days of the Lord of Misrule, for the dignified proceedings of prize-giving were punctuated by all manner of remarks shouted from the gallery and aimed not only at the students but the professors as well. Dr. Body, who succeeded Provost Whitaker in 1881, put a stop to the time-worn proceeding, but in Lampman's day it was still flourishing with vigour. One particular Convocation was remembered ever after by the freshmen. As a fortification against nervousness, they proceeded to the meeting in a body and were conducted by the grave-faced usher to their places at the top of the hall, there to establish themselves coolly. It occurred to them that the graduates were staring unduly, that the fair faces in the hall had assumed a wondering look, but they took these and the outburst of glee from the demons in the gallery as their merited meed. But they were all blushes and humiliation when they found upon the arrival of the Dean that they were occupying the chief seats destined for the fathers of the University even then waiting to file in, in all the grandeur of hood and gown.

Yet such moments had their value in creating that common bond whereby, in sheer self-defence, the freshmen class developed an *esprit de corps* and its members began to make friends with one another. At a later Convocation when Lampman went forward to receive his honours the boys chanted from the gallery:

> "There goes Lampman the first of the lot,
> A walking edition of Liddle and Scott."

One of the first things that Lampman did after entering college as a freshman was to join the Trinity College Literary Institute. This institution was really older than the college, since it had had its inception in 1849 in a debating society for the members of the Theological School at Cobourg, from which the Divinity School of Trinity University later sprang. The ceremony of becoming an Institute member was a distinct ordeal for Lampman. He was conducted into a large room by two ushers appointed for the purpose. The walls were lined with-amused and none too decorous students. It was necessary to perform various evolutions to their intense amusement. Then he shook hands with the grinning chairman and the still more widely grinning secretary. Finally he attempted to make a speech, which was interpolated with extremely candid criticism from the body of the hall. Speech-making was decidedly not in his line, and yet he took part in at least one Institute debate of which he has left an account. On that occasion he sat with five others on a dais. Before him was a sea of faces among which whiskers appeared to predominate. His auditors seemed the very acme of criticism. When he arose he felt a melancholy shivering in his knees, and his carefully prepared speech seemed to be fading away into a few stammered words arranged about as correctly as the geological specimens in the College Museum.

He was doubtless much more successful in the position of Institute librarian, which necessitated his presence on certain days in the week when the library was opened for members to borrow books. These were of the more popular type, and the library throve until the opening of a public library made its existence no longer necessary.

The Institute also managed the annual conversazione and possessed the inestimable privilege of presenting free tickets. The conversazione of 1883 goes down in history as the first to introduce dancing, but in Lampman's day the entertainment took the form of a concert and promenade. This, however, was the one activity of the Institute which did not much interest him. To be sure, there were his sisters to be taken, but for himself he found college functions rather upsetting and a bore.

The Institute met weekly for debates, readings and music, and the procedure was in pseudo-parliamentary form. But never was there a greater lack of order in any meeting or profounder ignorance of the correct manner of conducting it. True, there was formality almost to the extent of the ridiculous, for a constitution ponderous from the accumulated revisions of numberless members only added to the heat of arguments arising from correct or incorrect rulings till several members would be on their feet at once, all quoting clauses *verbatim*. Moreover, further revisions were always being proposed and opposed. To Lampman, especially during his freshman year the meeting of the Institute was vastly attractive. Never had he seen such ritual, or felt such party spirit, or listened to such forensic eloquence. Certainly there had been nothing like it at Port Hope.

He always recalled his freshman days with pleasure, "the transition" he called it, "from strict school discipline—the rude tyranny of master, cane and imposition hanging depressingly over the head of the marble-playing urchin, to the sudden and dazzling glory of college freedom and embryo manhood. How cloudlessly happy we were in those days, when the broad paternal protection still hung soothingly over us, shutting out with its obvious shadow all the real ties of future existence, when the ancestral coin still jingled safely in our capacious pockets, before the ominous 'Little Go' had brought the first darking shadow, sobering us a little, and the final approach of bachelorhood—grand consummation of all things—had reminded us of the inexorable stride of time, bringing sad glintings of coming labour and care, mingled with pressing doubts of a future sufficiency of most necessary bread and butter."

Almost before he knew it, the Christmas holidays had come and gone Then he returned to the still novel life of the College, to skating, to tramps along the snowy streets during the long Canadian winter, to his classical courses and his wider reading in English literature, to his new friends with their engrossing chats about everything under the sun, to all the warmth and activity and infinite variety which made college life pleasant to the boy who had always been so quiet but who was beginning to launch out into new fields of sociability and reading and discussion.

When spring came, bringing with it examinations, Lampman showed that in spite of these new activities he had not fallen behind in his work, and he received the Wellington Scholarship for that year.

With the reassembling of College in the autumn of 1880 there was a new spirit in the air, an immense excitement on the part of certain student *literati*. A birthday was approaching, the birthday of "Rouge et Noir." This first venture in Trinity College journalism was named from the college colours, and the progenitors were Travers Lewis, W. M. Cruttenden, and F. E. Howitt. The first number was a private venture but succeeded so well that it was at once taken over by the men in residence who were quick to see the advantage of an organ which, with characteristic frankness, could express their views and voice their complaints as well as provide a means of publication for the various prose efforts and poems, prize and otherwise, which were continually being produced. There were protests against the unheated corridors, the broken condition of the fence, the apathy of the College fathers towards the fight against non-religious education and the chaotic condition of the Institute meetings. It is not much wonder that the authorities at times grew a little uneasy and that there were rumors of suppression. But after all, the real emphasis was put upon the literary side of the periodical.

Lampman's first appearance in the columns of the paper was in the December issue, 1880, with a discussion of Shelley's "Revolt of Islam." Though suffering slightly from extravagant adjectives, the criticism is first hand; there is a real feeling for versification and imagery, and the writing is not self-conscious. He points out how Shelley's sensitive nature was turned in upon itself by the evils of society, how a strange perversion of understanding through atheism closed "Queen Mab" to many Christian ears, how the "Revolt of Islam" was written to counteract Shelley's depression over the failure of the French Revolution. "What first strikes the reader of Shelley and fills him with wonder," he says, "is the extraordinary profusion, variety and splendor of his imagery. An unpoetical reader is dazzled and bewildered by it, and a careless one pronounces it obscure and unreadable, and throws the book aside. But the student and admirer of Shelley turns the pages of his favorite author at random and is continually enchanted by the marvelous succession of magnificent pictures which every stanza opens before his eyes; an imagery bold, grand, profuse, but never strained, never out of place."

His second contribution to "Rouge et Noir" appeared in the issue of February, 1881, and was entitled "Friendship." It takes as its text a quotation from Carlyle: "Friendship in the old historic sense of the term no longer exists; it is, in reality, no longer expected or recognized as a virtue among men." Lampman's contention is that civilization as it advances over the ruins of the past becomes ruthless, and he finds in selfishness the curse of modern society. Thus, "he who rushes into the great world, restless with its countless multitudes of cold, selfishly struggling, ever-changing human beings," need not expect to find a friend who will give him counsel in prosperity and comfort in distress. Let him seek one rather, "who cares little for the world and knows less, one who never ventures to elbow his way among the merciless crowd, whose heart is unclouded by its sophistries, whose feelings are free to turn the way that nature would lead them."

This is strange thinking for a young man of nineteen, and the writing is still stranger in its self-conscious tone, its picture of brothers separated and estranged in the vast Babel of life, its heavy moralizing, and the recurrence of the bitter world theme. The explanation is not apparent. Was it an echo of the melancholy of Romanticism? Was it due to his ancestry and the fondness of Teutonic literature which even at Trinity College School was beginning to interest him? Was he congenitally sad; or was it simply the Wertherism of sensitive youth? It is possible that personal experience had to do with such a mood. He was rich in friends at College, but his lack of money would have been very galling to a less philosophic youth and no doubt bothered him. Moreover, sensitive and idealistic as he was, he shrank from the thought of battling for a living in the world. He was positive, courageous, even aggressive in manner with people of his own sort, but his college days were intermittently haunted with the thought of the commercial struggle that was to come. Perhaps something may be due to the fact that at his age youth is frequently more sophisticated than in later life and feels the burdens of the whole world upon its young shoulders. But throughout his life-time Lampman always entertained this dislike and fear of commercialism, and shunned contact with its blighting effects. He had these melancholy moments in youth, and the letters of his last years are tinged with depression and despair.

His interest in German literature led to the writing of an article on "German Patriotic Poetry" which appeared in "Rouge et Noir" for March, 1882. It is remarkable for distinct German bias, and for the quotation of poetry so patriotic but so unliterary that it is difficult to believe it selected by the man who had so recently been writing comparatively judicious criticism of Shelley. His plea was that its rude fervor placed it outside the bounds of exacter criticism. He distinguishes between French and German courage, the former as egotistic and flaming, the latter grounded upon duty and glowing like a steady fire. He finds this same quality of steadfastness and affection in the German war songs and mentions the pathetic vein so often running through them. Ten years later, when he wrote literary criticism for the *Globe*, his opinion of Shelley had become less enthusiastic, but his views of German literature and character remained practically unchanged.

Through the medium of "Rouge et Noir," Lampman was gradually becoming known among undergraduates and alumni as a writer of prose criticism. But he made no great impression, and other men were writing for the paper quite as well and more frequently. As yet he had published no verse; the prize poems during his time were written by others. As a talker and companion, however, his reputation spread, and he was a welcome visitor to any room in the college. He could not have been said to have the gift of leadership, but he had a singular faculty of appealing to many different types. He became intimate with few, but he had a charm of manner and a real gift for animated discussion which made him universally liked and easily one of the most popular men in the college in his day.

Moreover, he had an unfailing sense of humor. He could make up the most amusing rhymes on the spur of the moment, and his talent for mimicry was priceless. At that time the professor of classics at Trinity was one of those characters whose doings and mannerisms are the talk of the place, becoming converted almost into a legend in the years after they are gone. This was Professor Boyes; "Little Boyes," they called him. He was a native of Somersetshire, an odd little man, the more amusing for his dialect. His interest in the college and students was boundless. Because he did not like the traditional college song "Metagona," supposed to have been introduced from some old German university by Professor Ambery, the first classical professor, he composed another, with both

Greek and Latin versions. He loved jokes, and the one which became historic occurred when a student, unable to go on in a recitation, asked for a translation and received the reply in broad Somersetshire dialect: "Ah, Mr. Doomble, the ox knoweth his owner, and the aass his maaster's crib."

Professor Boyes' rooms were in the main building on the second floor at the east end where the corridor turned toward "The Wilderness." Above the second floor was an immense, unfinished attic, access to which was had by a small trap door in the ceiling of "The Coffin," a room so named from its shape and size. One night, being bored with life, a party of boys, which included Lampman, squirmed up into the murky vastness of this cavern beneath the roof. Picking their way carefully along the timbers, they presently came to a brick wall which had to be surmounted, and proceeded in a southerly direction till one of them discovered another manhole. Careful investigation proved this to be in the ceiling of the hall just outside Professor Boyes' rooms. Then Lampman had an inspiration. Opening the trap door just enough for him to be heard but not seen, his entertainment began. Soon Professor Boyes heard floating down from the roof something very like his own voice in chapel chanting in ludicrous Somersetshire dialect one of his favorite passages, "Woe unto thee, Chorazin. Woe unto thee, Bethsaida." The professor was also not ungifted as a singer, and although he could only pick out a tune with one finger on his little melodion, he sometimes amused himself by singing to that accompaniment. Accordingly the next number on the attic programme was Lampman's interpretation of the Boyesian rendition of "Wait till the clouds roll by, Jennie," accompanied by stifled snickers from above. Unable to stand it longer, the Professor rushed out, noted the empty rooms, and next morning there was a series of fines for the participants in the impromptu concert.

As time went on, with closer friendship, wider reading and literary activity, it is evident from his account of an imaginary student, in reality himself, that Lampman became less and less a grinder. Mounting to his room after a hearty tea and a short romp in the music room, he would resolve to work all the evening. The door would be carefully bolted, the fire lighted, tobacco shoved out of reach, Greek lexicon opened and study begun. "Surely he is lost for good and all," says Lampman, "in the dream of dead poets, and the lingering music of that soft, sonorous old dead tongue that men shall never forget. What a vision of this little monotonous college world shall now charm always his soul in the entrancing agony of Œdipus, the deep, wise, god-like voice of Antigone, and the vast poetry, the sweet, stormy imagery of the Sophoclean chorus—surely none." But soon his thoughts and then his eyes begin to wander. He rises and seats himself in front of the grate and gazes into "that fascinating fire-world cut into every form of mountain, glen and palace turret, fashioned for the very unchaining of the fancies of men." Alas, he has lighted his pipe. "A sound of cheery voices calling invitations to each other out in the corridor thrills him, and a moment after he hears a clattering of active heels down, down to the clanking stones of the buttery—it is the sound of some merry irresistible cheese-god rapping at the very threshold of his stomach." There is a knock, and he opens the door. "A head, just a black curly head and the gleam of full laughing lips appears: 'You miserable old grinder, come round and have a glass of beer.' Œdipus is dead; the clouds are hurled away from his tomb, and everything is sweet and serene."

To judge from the reminiscences of the Trinity men of those days, body and soul were kept together chiefly by means of bread and beer and cheese. The beer was sold in the buttery at ten cents a jug, but connoisseurs preferred the beverage bottled by Messrs. Labatt and O'Keefe. This resulted in the accumulation of quantities of beer bottles, and it was a favorite practice to collect these for proper removal. Long after lights were out at eleven, a doleful dirge would begin to resound through the halls and a group of dark figures would be seen solemnly pacing along and carrying in their midst something which was supposed to be a corpse, but which looked very much more like a gown filled with empty bottles. When a professor's door had been reached these would be suddenly dumped against it with a great clatter, but by the time the master had looked out all the "mourners" would have fled.

All this time Lampman was not simply loafing and visiting and playing college pranks, but had continued to try his hand at verse. His first productions are interesting when compared with his prose and poetry of later years. "Verses" which appeared in "Rouge et Noir" for February, 1882, is probably his first published poem. It is constricted in movement and depressingly moralistic, with its picture of Man submerged by the waves of Fate.

His prose writing at the time is illustrated by an article on Gambetta in "Rouge et Noir" for July, 1883. It is written in a free and flowing style not before noticeable in Lampman's prose and exemplified in his description of the old days in France, "when two hundred and fifty-eight forges went clanging through the autumn days in all the open places of Paris, and shone lurid, gleaming with their sooty Vulcans about them through the long nights hammering musket barrels and tempering sabres, hour by hour; when, to save time in bringing them down, the bells were shot from the steeples with heavy guns to make the patriots' cannon, and every cellar was raked to get them saltpetre, when all souls that could hold a musket gathered in the towns and villages and wended away to the battle-field chanting the *Marseillaise;* when the bands of girls and old women grew weary scraping lint and sewing canvas night and day, and the old men sat like veterans in the market places, giving benediction to the heroes that were to fight for *la Patrie;* when bread and fire-locks were deemed the only two requisites for victory—such old time they (the French of the '70's) remembered but dimly, for the spirit had left them long ago." This spirit Gambetta had been obliged to revive, and Lampman, influenced perhaps by Carlyle, grew eloquent in describing the attempt.

The subject of this article, the prose discussion of German war poetry, and a long Franco-Prussian war poem, "The Last Sortie," in "Rouge et Noir," November, 1882, indicate that Lampman's imagination was fired in these days by certain aspects of militarism—an interest which may possibly be attributed to his loyalist ancestors. It is evident also from a comparison of his poetry in this period with the fluent prose of his essays and letters written at the time, that Lampman the prose writer somewhat preceded Lampman the poet in the volume and character of his earliest work.

One of the events looked forward to eagerly in the year at Trinity was the reading, usually on some night in February, of the annual message from Father Episcopon. No one knows how long this semi-deity had resided in the "pepper box" belfry till his alleged discovery in 1858 by Pakenham Edward Stewart, who with Joel Bradbury and George T. Carruthers undertook to convey his message to the college by means of "The Episcopon," an annual communication read by the Scribe or editor. Each year the Scribe, who was selected by his predecessor, would post up a notice to the effect that Father Episcopon had been heard from, and that contributions would be received from students and even from professors. The material thus collected endeavored to correct any shortcomings or eccentricities of the men, was humorous and satiric, and frequently very frank. Only those contributions showing personal animosity were barred by the editors, who were a mysterious body of three, secretly appointed by the out-going editors, and who made themselves known to the Scribe, the only other person in the college who knew their indentity.

One Saturday evening in March, 1881, the college was duly notified to assemble in Lampman's room, for he was the Scribe for that year. By this time he had moved to the front of the main building toward the eastern end not far from Professor Boyes' rooms, where his windows looked out through the oaks to Queen Street beyond. It was past the hour when lights were out, and the only illumination was from the fire and a single candle, which stood on a lectern flanked by a gruesome, grinning skull while gleaming in the corner was the least ethereal materialization which Father Episcopon was ever known to assume—the college skeleton. When all had assembled, under-graduates, a graduate or two, but never a professor, Lampman rose and began to read. One sees him very clearly, his delicate skin, oval face, his brown hair a little curly and worn rather long, his fine features in the light of the candle as clear-cut as a cameo. He read in a clear soft voice, purposely without much emphasis. There was an introduction, the Scribe's account of his interview with Father Episcopon and parodies in the metre of the "Ancient Mariner," "Hiawatha," and of the classics, in making which he was an adept. The popularity of Gilbert and Sullivan was also reflected, and Shakespeare was drawn upon for apt quotation. Each quip was greeted with roars of laughter by all but the one satirized. From time to time the company would burst into a college song, the beer and bread and cheese would be passed afresh, and the reading begun again. One of the most interesting features of Lampman's work as Scribe was the drawings, "etchings" he called them, which besprinkled his pages. They not only were drawn with skill but showed powers of caricature and a keen sense of the ludicrous. This writing and drawing had taken a good deal of time, but it probably gave him more pleasure than anything else he did at college, and when the meeting broke up it was generally agreed that Lampman was the best Scribe in years. The result was that the next two volumes in November, 1881, and March, 1882, were prepared by him.

"Episcopon" and "Rouge et Noir" took so much of Lampman's time that his work suffered somewhat. Moreover, his mind was full of literary plans due to his association in college with his friend, J. A. Ritchie, and in the city with J. E. Collins, journalist and later biographer, and Charles G. D. Roberts, poet and editor, whose volume of poems, "Orion," stimulated Lampman's own poetic gifts. With these men he sometimes visited Toronto friends, who were greatly entertained by the animated talk of the three friends, their eager interest in the new poetry, Roberts' plans for Canadian journalism, and arguments about the conflict of science and religion in the days when Darwin and Huxley were so much read and when doubt and skepticism seemed in the very air.

When spring came in 1882, it was necessary for him to get down to work. There were visions of strong tea and wet towels as aids to Greek cramming. But what a temptation there was in the long golden afternoons to chat under the oaks or go "rambling through the jingling summer town, or up the ravine walks, shaded from the heat or sound; or westward to the lake, the park and the Humber." At night "the teasing insects would swarm in from the cool moonlit ravine and a drunken crazy pinch-bug butt the windowpane or fling himself recklessly round the gas-lit room."

And so he who might have won a first was glad, in the final examination, to get a second. Yet he had not been idle. He had developed immensely through reading, discussion and thought. More than anything, he had profited by his friends. That is why he said: "But the deepest reason why college reminiscences must always linger very pleasantly in the heart of every man who has not grown to be a mere money-making automaton is that friendships, as lasting and genuine as any can be, are formed there—friendships which grow together strangely and unaccountably, founded variously, some few upon similarity of disposition, many upon similarity of tastes and pursuits, most of all upon some mysterious sympathy which he did not understand and never shall. So that in these after years he may look about him and feel that he is not utterly alone in the measureless waste, that there are still one or two who would be glad to meet him again, who would cheerfully help him if he were in need, nay, would perhaps sacrifice much in his behalf."

In the Trinity College "Review" for February, 1888, appeared the following otherwise unpublished sonnet—a tribute to his college friends:

GENTLEMEN

"Ah, brothers of sweet thought, so rare to find,
Men of the gentle soul and gentle speech,
Toward whom out of these droughty sands we reach
Hot hearts that hunger for your summer wind.
Full of sweet help, forever frank and kind,
Blessed are ye for this high truth ye teach,
That life hath yet some radiant good for each,
Nor all its ways nor all its thought gone blind.

Not to the strong, earth's iron-visaged lords,
Shall gift from us nor any praise be due;
Rather with longing lips we bend to you
Uttering your names with soft and reverent words.
Earth's simple children, perfect in your part,
Near to your own and to our mother's heart."

CHAPTER V.

TEACHING SCHOOL.

WITH College over, Lampman was now without definite occupation, and a shortage of funds made it necessary that he turn his hand to something. He had an excellent education and had always been so surrounded with teachers and teaching, at home and elsewhere, that a schoolmaster's position was naturally the first to suggest itself. Moreover, teacher-training courses were not then required, and a man might go directly into the profession from college. While still without a position, he wrote the following letter to his college friend, J. A. Ritchie of Ottawa:

283 Jarvis Street,
Toronto, July 24, 1882.

John of Ottawa,

I have heard naught from thee or of thee. When thou leavest thy friends and travellest into remote parts, it would be decent of thee to leave them some slight clue whereby they might know whether thou art well and prosperous or the reverse. I have been so knocked about and disturbed during these few weeks of July that I have done no grinding as yet, though I have written many letters and poems—the former to various secretaries of school boards (all Scotchmen, I observe) throughout this fertile province—the latter for my own special amusement and delectation. Touching the school matter, I have applied to Orillia, Vankleek Hill (refused there!); Orangeville and Stratford ($900 a year, impossible!) Orangeville is the one I think I shall get. The

Rev. A. Henderson, who hath the cure of souls in that rising village and hath, besides, it seems, which is more to the point, a considerable influence with the august board (of blockheads), wrote an obliging letter to the pink of the Joneses:(1) *requiring of him the name of some Trinity man who would accept of the position. Jones referred him to me, and I presently received a letter from the Reverend the Cure asking if I was at liberty to take upon me the weight of this sublime jurisdiction. I wrote an obliging letter in return, assuring the Priest that I had no objection to the situation and would graciously accede to his proposal, since the country was apparently in such urgent need of my services. I have not yet had his answer, but I expect it will be favorable.*

Touching the poetical works of Archibald Lampman, first series, I have composed, I think, four since I last saw you. From writing an essay in commendation of German Patriotic poetry, I have proceeded to deeper depravity and written an addition to that patriotic poetry myself—entitled "The Last Sortie." Another is the completion of the verses I began about Coecina and the Roman Legions in the wastes of the Longes Pontes. It now numbers 45 stanzas, "The Little Minstrel" and the "Preacher" are titles of the others, the latter being the best thing I have yet written. If you will deign to answer this letter, I will send you a bunch of my verses, but not otherwise. You will see some improvement, I think; for I have been very careful with these last poems, spending more time on the correcting than on the original writing. The more I write the more I see that Roberts' objections were glaringly just, and that those first things I sent to him and read to you are strung together with lamentable slovenliness. I sent two poems "Last Sortie" and "Shelley," to "Our Continent" and "Harper," re-

---

(1) Rev. Wm. Jones, B.A., Scholar of St. John's College, Cambridge, and Professor of Mathematics at Trinity.

spectively—got 'em back (promptly). I'm afraid "Our Continent" is a clique business. I see the same names every time. Collins is trying it with a light prose article. I await the result with curiosity. I have more to say to you, but will reserve for another letter, conditional upon your answering this.

Yours in sympathy,

A. Lampman.

On August 4th, 1882, he wrote to the same friend from Thorold, Ontario, in the Niagara District, where he had gone to visit his uncle, Mr. Frederick Lampman, who was a barrister there: "I have been accepted by the parliament of Orangeville and shall, on the first of September, take my seat in the Cabinet. This continually writing applications is at length over—it was getting monotonous. I learned a regular formula by heart, and whensoever I saw an advertisement in the papers I sat me down incontinently and wrote a series of set phrases considerably eulogistic of myself." Then followed anticipations of future beer-drinking evenings at the college, news of Collins' writing activities, and plans about the management of 'Rouge et Noir'. Of himself, he continued: "I sent an article to 'Forest and Stream.' The scoundrels wrote to me saying that they were very much pleased with my performance, but they were not buying (orders of their publishers); that, however, they will, if I like, print it and send me their cursed paper, in return, for a year. Though I don't want it, I wrote and said yes, for I knew not what to do with the article else."

The article entitled "Fishing in Rice Lake" appeared in "Forest and Stream" on August 10th, 1882, and was a vivid, though somewhat wordy, account of a fishing trip undertaken by Lampman and a fat old gentleman, with "a tough denizen of the neighbourhood" to pull the oars.

On August 22nd he was back again at the Jarvis Street house in Toronto writing that his friend Collins had made friends with the distinguished man of letters, Goldwin Smith, and dined with him on Sunday. There were proposals for Collins to work on the *Telegram* newspaper and on a literary monthly, plans for which the great man was hatching. Collins told him that the literary people he met at Goldwin Smith's dinner-table spoke of Swinburne as "poor" Swinburne, and that, from what he gathered, the poet was rapidly sinking into the condition of a confirmed, debilitated drunkard. Of his own work he said:

I am not going to be bothered giving my productions excursions to New York and Boston and back any more, but shall look forward to publishing them in a lump some day. I have made acquaintance with a little German musician here named Carl Martens, for whom I have composed an amorous song which he will put to music. He wants me to undertake with him the composition of a comic opera. Hurrah! . . . I have been thinking lately that something might be done with short sketches, descriptions of character and like in the manner somewhat of Dickens—subjects such as 'Village Life,' 'Musical Professors' ('School boards!'), etc.

The letter closed with the poem beginning "I saw a proud ship, tall and gay," an allegory dealing in moralizing vein with the subject of a shipwrecked life, later published in "Rouge et Noir" under the title of "Derelict."

August was soon past, and September 1st found Lampman in Orangeville. It was a trying time, as the letters of the period very well show. On September 9th he wrote from the Gordon House Hotel to his friend:

"Here endeth the first week of pedagogy and right tired

I am of it too. John of Ottawa, take the advice of one whose eyes have been terribly opened, never descend to the abyss of pedagogy if there is another path open in any direction to thee in this life. This one week has shorn me of my flesh, my sleep and my appetite, and I am but the merest unwholesome residue even of what I was. Here I have found but one civilized man, the head-master of my school, Alexander Steele, and if it had not been for his civility and the pleasure of his countenance and conversation I should undoubtedly have cut and run several days ago and sought a more congenial clime. As it is, however, I am partially resigned to my lot. The school is not one of a high order, it is of a decidedly low character, and has a bad reputation for unruly students. However, I have had no difficulty so far with the bigger fellows, except that I find it devilish hard to discover what they know. It is the little brutes that bother me. Last Friday (yesterday) I gave them a solemn warning that they had better turn over a new leaf, and next week, DEO VOLENTE, *I shall lay out 25 cents in the way of a cane; possibly that may induce order to come out of chaos. I teach Latin, Greek, English Literature, History and German. You should hear me lecturing on Scott's 'Marmion' to about thirty big boys, or rather men and girls, most of them a head taller than I am, and able, if they choose, to pitch me out of the window, each one of them with his left hand. You should hear my earnest endeavours to make the rustic lips get round the mysteries of the German dipthongs or accomplish a row of ch's."*

Life in Orangeville was made tolerable only by the kindness of the Principal, letters from friends, and the anticipation of returning to the St. Simon and St. Jude's dinner at Trinity in October. But the date of the dinner was changed, and occasioned the following lament to his friend:

"I have rest (sic) my soul in the hope of having a grand

evening on that day—now I am thrown back into the God-forsaken gloom of a month of Orangeville thoughts. Here I shall have to sit on Saturday night like Tantalus, my jaws watering to their roots with the unutterable vision of oysters, poultry, nuts, raisins, wines, toasts, speeches, and songs sweeter than all, cursing my fate and filled with ravening bitterness. John of Ottawa, I mean to quit this teaching business as soon as possible. I can't stand it any longer."

After a month at Orangeville, the much dreaded date of October 1st arrived, and Lampman sat for his final examinations. He had not studied as hard at college as at school, the summer had been unsettled by indefinite arrangements for the future, and finally had come a month of the most difficult kind of teaching for a man untrained and unsuited in temperament for the profession. In spite of these handicaps, his excellent foundation in the classics stood him in good stead. It is said that some of the translation he did at sight. At any rate he passed with second class honours and was pleased with the result.

He continued his teaching with difficulty but appeared at a teachers' convention of which he wrote an amusingly exaggerated account:

"I read an essay last Saturday before the assembled army of pedagogues—web-footed, English-mutilating, spoon-in-cup, knife-instead-of-fork-substituting, tobacco-chewing barbarians from every quarter of the county—it took very well—wonderfully well, I may say. An old, fat, spectacled pedagogue of the most genuine stamp got up to criticize it and by way of criticizing it he started to give a complete historical, critical and philological account of the Indo-Germanic languages and had got as far as the time of Alfred the Great when the chairman shut him up and obliged him to sit down.

"My school work is wearing, and I have hard work to preserve order. My little boys are very unruly—the other

day I assaulted and bitterly allbestrapped one of them, inasmuch that along the close-wrought desks and well-polished benches there passed a great hush, like the hush of the sea when the storm hath swept over it. It lasted about an hour, and the disorder began again. The Pedagogue, like the poet, is born and not made—I am beginning to realize that fact, and propose at the end of the year to make a strike for something more in my line. I have the greatest mind in the world at the first opportunity to settle to work in Toronto, get any kind of writing that I can, and go in with all my might, make or break."

Long after he left Orangeville Lampman continued to entertain grave doubts as to whether literature could be taught.

"*In our Canadian schools,*" he wrote, "*we undertake to teach literature and we certainly do teach it with a vengeance. We have bulky grammars, awful and discouraging to the eye; elaborate books instructive of the art of composition; carefully prepared editions of classical English writings with explanatory notes, historical notes, glossaries, critical introductions and so forth. Armed with these, our literature classes are set upon the study of some particular masterpiece—say, a book of 'Paradise Lost.' They read it; they declaim it rhetorically; they get it by heart; they analyze it sentence by sentence; they parse it word for word; they study its language syllable by syllable; following each word to its remotest kindred in Latin, Greek, Saxon, old High German, Lithuanian and Sanskrit; they turn it into prose and back again into verse; they hunt up all the allusions; they make themselves acquainted with the parallel passages; they discuss it historically, geographically, critically; they tear and worry and torture the lines of the great poem till they are littered out as dry and innutritive as a worm-eaten codfish. When all this has been done, the student's mind is perhaps accuter for the mental training, but he wishes never to hear the name of 'Paradise Lost' again. It is indeed a Paradise lost to him. And not only have the power and beauty of one English masterpiece been destroyed to his ear, but the chances are that his faculty of appreciation generally has been robbed of its natural freshness and permanently blunted. Whatever may be the merit of this system as an intellectual exercise for the young, it is decidedly not the way to cultivate a love of literature or the power of producing it. Indeed, it seems to me that to teach literature in the schools by classes is as impossible as it would be to teach morality in the same way. The love of literature is a natural gift, and if not strong enough to develop itself can only be drawn out by the influence of a certain surrounding intellectual atmosphere and the magic af literary companionship."*

He felt that the study of literature in the universities tended to produce scholars and even pedants, and as the professors must study the whole scholarly background they usually lacked artistic attainment. He suggested that a sort of literary lecturing guild might be formed composed of travelling lecturers more in touch with the creative literary world.

Any attempt to write during his stay in Orangeville must have been a great effort. Teaching taxed his energy, which was never great, and more than anything, he lacked associates and inspiration. In a letter dated December 14th he said: "*Believe me, John of Ottawa, I* FRETTED *more over my utter inability to send you anything than I can describe. I strained away day after day with pen and paper bodily before me, but without avail. Thou canst guess what ailed me. It was weeks since I heard the thunder of trains in the Union Station, the din of many feet on the stone pavements of King Street and, above all, the joyous voices of mine own old acquaintances and never forgotten friends. After a week's absence from these scenes, I grow too dull to put pen to paper, save in the correcting of some sweet-faced urchin's exercise.*"

It was at this time that Lampman was offered a position as clerk in the Post Office Department at Ottawa through his college friend, Archibald Campbell, whose father Sir Alexander Campbell, was Postmaster General of Canada. The salary was not large, but the position offered an escape from teaching into the less exacting routine of a government office, where short hours would give some time for writing, though, of course, Lampman's almost unknown literary aspirations had nothing to do with his appointment to the office. He accepted gladly, and left Orangeville and the teaching profession at the close of school in December.

CHAPTER VI.

OTTAWA.

HE Christmas of 1882 Lampman spent with his family in the Jarvis Street house in Toronto. There were many tales to be told of his recent experiences in Orangeville. He would have tea with Campbell, who seemed lonely and not at all satisfied with the Law, and many long communings with Collins over past writings and future plans. On January 11th he left for Ottawa, and soon after was at work as a temporary clerk in the Post Office Department, from which he wrote:

P. O. Dept.,
Ottawa.

John of Ottawa: *January 19.*

This is a place not of "wind and flowers, full of sweet trees and colour of glad grass," but a place of chill fierce colds, full of rheumatism and damned snowstorms. I fear the coloured glory of the Parliament Buildings will be covered up with a hundred feet of snow-banks to-morrow morning, for the heaven and the earth are filled to-night with one sheet of dim drifting white. I am in the Savings Bank branch of the P. O. Department, and am pretty busy with easy monotonous work, the same thing over and over from January to December. Hours easy and time to myself, thank God. Had the devil's own time finding a place to board. The near approach of sessions makes it particularly hard. However, I succeeded at last and not by any means badly. I shall write again presently.

Your affte. friend,
A. Lampman.

There are two post-scripts to this letter. The first is pictorial and represents himself seated on a very high stool at a very high desk writing with great determination. The other is a quatrain written apropos of the wintry night:

> "Down the dim white gusty wastes that waken
> With no sound of wheels or tramp of feet,
> Grey thin whirling mists of snow are shaken
> Through the strong tall towers and soundless street."

At this time Ritchie sold a poem to the "Continent," and his friend was characteristically eager to congratulate him. Of his own work he wrote:

"*I have grown wonderfully prolific of verse since I came here. I sent two winter poems to Collins and have almost done polishing three more—all of them of some length. I wrote forty-eight lines last night and got into such a fever over it that I couldn't sleep all night. I have the long evenings to myself and invariably fall adreaming, which always ends in the shooting of a new subject across my brain. . . . My verse is continually getting better, I am glad to say, so that I shall probably send you, in a day or two, a copy of verses which I am somewhat proud of. I hope you will also send me some evidence of your industry before long. I am belching forth like a volcano: do thou the same. . . .*

"*. . . Last week I mailed one of my winter pieces to the 'Canadian Illustrated News', and I suppose if they accept it it will be printed in this week's number. If they don't accept it, it will certainly be the unkindest welt of all and the very last hair, etc., and I shall infallibly buy a revolver.*"

But purchase of fire-arms was unnceessary, for the paper accepted and published the poem, "Winter Evening," on February 3rd, 1883. The metre and diction are somewhat stilted, but the flaming sun, setting behind dull clouds, the misty stars, the snow crunching under foot, are indicative of the poetry which was to come.

Lampman's tastes and occupations at the time are further illustrated by the following extract from one of his letters: "*I have been dreaming a great deal lately, sitting in the evenings with my pipe between my teeth, in an armchair, Matthew and Swinburne at my elbow and Shelley on my knee. But I shall have to give it all up now at once and set to work on shorthand. For many months you shall get no more verse or prose from me. The novel, which has become a pet scheme with me and much of the matter of which has been fermenting in my head, must be abandoned for this year any way. I am in a very good condition for verse making, as I am altogether undisturbed through the long evenings. The one thing I lack is a private room to write in, which is, of course, beyond my means. However, shorthand must be my Literature for some time to come. I like the Civil Service. I get enough to eat. I have not seen the Library. My boarding place is not exactly a 'boarding house,' as I am the only boarder and have things entirely to myself. I go to work at 9.30, taking lunch with me; get away at four, have dinner at six, and do nothing the rest of the time. If I had no shorthand to bother me, I believe I should write a good sized volume of verse in the next six months. I am getting a most comfortable ease of versification nowadays from continual practice, which removes every hindrance from my way. . . . I have betaken me lately back to my old love, Shelley, and I swear that he is the greatest of them all. There is a sort of tremendous, weird, unearthly majesty in his wilder pieces which no one had ever approached, and in his sweeter ones a fancy so delicate and fairy-like as to be altogether astonishing, and out of the range of any other man's work that ever lived. You ought to read the 'Witch of Atlas.' It is not very long, and it is utterly indescribable.*"

These were happy, quiet days for Lampman, with time

for reading and thinking and writing poetry. But there were times when he was so busy with some office schedule or the study of shorthand that he wrote no letters to anyone for a month. There were times, too, when the elation from increasingly better composition gave way to dejection at the seeming uselessness of it all. Fortunately these moods did not last long. For instance, in another letter of this period he said:

"*About a week ago I made a solemn covenant with myself never to write another verse again, or construct a line of prose. This I did in all earnestness of despair, being entirely convinced of my ridiculous self-conceit and vanity and the utter real meanness of my abilities. I felt very gloomy for a few days, but, though I am more than half convinced still of the absurdity and futility of my castles in the air, yet I have already broken the covenant.*

"*Good or ill—poetry is to some men like the magnetic sea mountain in the Arabian Nights, that drew the very nails out of the ships to their distraction. This same delusion will doubtless ruin me, unfitting me for any solid profession, and yet in the end fulfilling none of the vapoury hopes I have founded upon it.*"

At other times he would write in great gayety. One of his favorite means of fun making was to launch into a terrible tirade behind which always lurked his shy smile of amusement. Such apparently was his mood on February 24th, 1883, when he wrote:

"*I have two pieces of important news, one joyful, one sad. 1. I have at length discovered a place where a thirsty man can get a glass of tolerably good beer, and I thank God for it. 2. Some rough, or roughs, has been so superfluous as to steal away mine ancient pipe, the grand old sufficient briar-root that Campbell gave me and which I had new-ambered last autumn. May the curse of Bacchus and Priapus follow him forever. May he be sick with every pipeful of it henceforward to all eternity. May he never be able to take more than three whiffs of any pipe without blistering his tongue. May he forever hunger and lust after a pipe when he cannot get it and have no taste for it when he has got it. May every ounce of the weed he buys turn to 'Gold Flake.' Having fulminated which solemn curses, I feel easy. I think they will take effect, I am so strong (sic) moved in the matter.*

"I am still toiling away at the 'Two Monks.' It is growing very long, and I have become disgusted with the butter-milk metre in which I was writing it, and have broken out wild into blank verse with stretches of the jingle in between. I propose to indulge in a few other variations of metre before I am done with it. I am unfortunately getting dull over the Monks. My present fit of mental activity is gradually dying out. I had one in June and July, you remember, which died out in October and November. Now I have had another which I feel is on the point of a second collapse. You may get little more from me until, say, May and June, when, I opine, my volcano will be ready for a third explosion. However there are, I should think, somewhere between two and three hundred lines of the Monks written—very roughly indeed, but yet in a state of advanced composition."

This poem, the story of a girl who, in the disguise of a monk, seeks her lover, is interesting as an early attempt at long narrative verse—a field which was popular at the time. In style and dramatic situation it has a certain power, but it is not Lampman at his best.

With the approach of examinations, Lampman began a series of warnings, half-serious, half-playful, to his friend:

"I hope, John, that you are grinding like a man and a soldier. You have now, as I calculate, barely four weeks to turn yourself in. Discard evening parties, which de-

moralize the flesh—keep moderate hours—shun the cricket field and particularly Scoles; (1) *a moderate draught of lager at 9.30 will suffice thee, together with a meagre portion of bread and cheese—keep thy door locked and permit not Jones* (2) *to occupy the coal box—shun the temptation of Scadding's;* (3) *have your text ever before you, your crib to the left and Lexicon to the right of you—let the tobacco jar rest on the mantle-piece, not on the table—if anybody knocks remain obdurately silent. These are the parting instructions of an old and experienced grinder. Let no untimely allurement of persons or sudden lust of the flesh disturb your calm regard for them, so shalt thou be the better prepared for the day of wrath to come, the great and bitter day of searchings, in the which shall be examined all things that be done in the body whether they be good or whether they be evil—the good being represented by clear head, well-worn crib and small lager bill—the evil by fear and trembling, beer bottles, Scadding and the Devil.*

"But in all earnestness, John, I hope you will be able to assure me in your next letter (and let it be speedily written) that you have buckled to work and are full of abstemiousness and diligence.

"I have one or two mild sets of verses in slow process of construction and am meditating a prose essay for the 'Atlantic Monthly', or some other like publication, also prose to contribute to next 'Rouge et Noir' as I did not the last."

At this time Lampman was living at 67 O'Connor Street, where he busied himself with reading and writing verse and prose, some of which found its way into "Rouge

---

(1) A Toronto athlete and keeper of a Yonge Street tavern.
(2) Wallace Jones, nephew of Professor Jones.
(3) Charles Scadding: Curate of St. George's, New York; Rector at the Grange, near Chicago; and Bishop of Oregon.

et Noir." For the "Canadian Illustrated News" he wrote a four-column review of his friend Collins' book, "The Life and Times of the Rt. Hon. Sir John A. McDonald."

It is evident that he depended very much in those days on the associations of College, for after an interval of eighteen days between letters he wrote:

"In the name of all the Devils what has befallen you, what has befallen Angell and 'R. et N.', what has befallen Shortt, what has befallen everybody? I have received no letter from any living soul of you for these two weeks.—See to it, John of Ottawa, see to it. You are now, as I imagine, immersed in the horrors of examination. I picture you with a towel round your head in the small hours perusing the fascinating pages of Hamlin Smith. Peruse, John, peruse without end. Work as if the whole seven devils of mathematics had entered into your garnished and swept apartments. Let no lager nor tobacco prevail over you in this, your supreme temptation in the wilderness. The Devil will not fail to take you up into a great tower and show you fair landscapes with vast groves of tobacco plants grown as big as plantains and far-echoing torrents of glittering, bubbling amber, foaming night and day—soft hazes, fragrant scents and winds breathing fragments of Matthew Arnold and Swinburne—fair gauzy maidens smoking cigarettes—birds, beasts, and creeping things with pipes in their mouths—milestones carven into the shape of hookahs with innumerable stems for the lame the halt and the blind—walking beer barrels perambulating the highways tobacco-shaded at all hours, fringed with well-cleaned schooners—all the forests and the gardens yield perpetual store of breads and delicate cheeses and divers kinds of cakes. But beware, for in the east, seaward from thy Mount of Carmel thou mayst see a cloud no larger than a man's hand, but which will grow with the speed of the whirlwind. In its bosom

are the chained lightnings which are Greek Iambics to slay thee, and the rolling thunder which is the voice of Hamlin Smith. Turn thine eyes away from the Devil, from the four hundred priests of Beelzebub, which is John Labatt and all his retainers, and from the slaying face of Jezebel, which is the fascination of fair women, and be as Ahab, repentant; gird up thy loins and run to thy palace ere the cloud hath overcast the heavens; slay the wicked priests which are the servants of Labatt, and turn thee to the ways of the Lord, which are the ways of Liddel and Scott, with all thy soul. Jesting aside, John, I hope you are working like a man and doing well. Never leave a paper till you have answered every single part of it about which you have the faintest knowledge. 'Have cheek, lest ye flunk,' is an invaluable motto. Follow it."

At certain times, such as the yearly balancing of the Department's books, he had little leisure or energy for composition, though Collins had commissioned him to write some descriptions of scenery for his next book, "Canada under the Administration of Lord Lorne." Often he felt the routine of the office irksome, though the work was not hard. For a time there was talk of his removal to the Department of Justice, possibly the Supreme Court Library, but nothing came of it. That he was sometimes discouraged and uncertain is indicated by the following:

"*I have a good many poems which I look on every day with increasing* DISGUST! *I shall have to betake myself to prose soon in self-defence in order to regain my peace of mind. My reading perpetually opens my mind more deeply to the fact that my poetical impulse is of a very pale and ordinary kind—the same sort of thing that hundreds of young men have felt and imagined themselves poets—nay, some have gone on imagining so till the end of their days—witness Bulwer, Jeffrey, Chateaubriand, etc. 'What is a poet?*

a corridor through which the wind RUSHES', *not in which there is an occasional draught. I sometimes manage in lucid moments to make clear to myself what a poet is: the sensation, or rather the imagination of the sensation, is something vast and makes one feel infinitely small. One is inclined to mistake a tendency to poetical forms of thought and poetical expression and intense appreciation of poetry, for creative gift—it isn't—that is, in a degree worth building upon. One may, however, turn that tendency to prose and let it comfort one, with high results. That is what I will do—as soon as I have found my subject.*"

Lampman was earnestly concerned at this time over Ritchie's preparation for examinations, and his letters are full of admonitions to study. They hoped to have a reunion with Campbell and Roberts in Toronto in the Fall regarding which he wrote: "*I shall visit you in October for three weeks, and we shall be all together there*—IO TRIUMPHE! *We shall occupy one end of a table at St. Simon and St. Jude's—the four of us—altogether for the oysters and the sherry and the tobacco—and the schemes we shall hatch there.* [A drawing of skull and cross-bones here follows.] *But alas, John! who dare speak of the morrow? Many a so delicious picture have I made, even as this, and have seen only a dark day and a weary hour come of it. Let us pray that it be not utterly so in this case.*"

It was about this time that the Lampmans decided to move from Toronto to Ottawa to be with their son, who seemed likely to remain permanently in Government service. The household consisted of Mr. and Mrs. Lampman, one daughter, who was making music a profession, and another, the "little sister" of the letters, who not only had literary aspirations but also a decided gift for painting. The Nicholas Street house into which they moved was a frame cottage, very small, but a pleasant place with an attractive garden. Lampman was delighted with the prospects of the change, and busied himself with all the details of moving and settling. Now he would have a room for himself to write as much as he wished; he would be able to indulge his old childhood fondness for gardening; more than all he would have the sympathetic companionship of the parents and sisters who had always been such an inspiration and delight.

"*I am getting settled here*," he wrote, "*as comfortably as my poverty will permit. Our house is a decidedly pleasant place at the corner of Nicholas and Theodore streets. Here we shall smoke pipes at Christmas and make ourselves merry in a small room which I intend to appropriate to my special use.*

"*I have done no work whatever yet, being too unsettled and too much worried with many things. Moreover, I have strained my back and arms with lifting things—scratched myself all over with nails—and caught half a dozen colds—and be damned to it all. My sister is less troubled with such things; she is exceedingly busy over another novelette. I begin to have hopes of her—she is 'little sister' no longer—having grown up into a woman in the last year—in fact since I saw her last—she is very bright and keeps my spirits up. We shall begin to work together—and help each other.*"

On December 6th, 1883, Charles G. D. Roberts brought out the first number of the weekly literary magazine called "The Week," which in excellence and interest was an outstanding achievement in the history of Canadian periodicals. The initial number was notable also in that it contained the first poem published by Lampman outside college circles. It was entitled "A Monition," though published later in "Among the Millet" as "The Coming of Winter."

"Out of the Northland sombre weirds are calling;
A shadow falleth southward day by day;
Sad summer's arms grow cold; his fire is falling;
His feet draw back to give the stern one way.

It is the voice and shadow of the slayer—
Slayer of loves, sweet world, slayer of dreams;
Make sad thy voice with sober plaint and prayer;
Make gray thy woods, and darken all thy streams.

Black grows the river, blacker drifts the eddy;
The sky is gray; the woods are cold below;
O make thy bosom and thy sad lips ready
For the cold kisses of the folding snow."

In the same paper, on January 17th, 1884, appeared "Three Flower Petals," the story of a little girl who had given him three petals of a sunflower for each of which he makes her a verse in return. It is a pretty poem, though somewhat sentimental.

His third contribution, in an entirely different mood and reminiscent of Poe, appeared on February 7th, 1884:

A FANTASY.

"As in a city given over to death,
One flying hour before the grave may be,
All frenzied mortals that have life and breath
Clasp hands, join lips, and take their fill of glee,—

The grave fulfils, and faster swirls the throng,
Redder the wine runs through the desperate days,
The dance grows louder, madder grows the song,
The kisses wilder as the blue plague slays:
So the leaves fall and death is wide to smite;
Haste, wind, make revel for a day and night."

These three poems are exceedingly significant in indicating, in contrast to his college verse, the rapid development which had taken place in Lampman's art: the widening of his interests in nature and humanity, and the increasing power and beauty of his versification.

During the winter of 1884, Collins went to Ottawa, where he worked on his book on the Lorne Administration. His visit was a godsend to Lampman, and the two friends smoked and talked and walked together, busy with numberless schemes of which Lampman wrote to Ritchie as follows: "*Last month, in pursuance and development of the meagre plan which I unfolded to you at Christmas, I set to work and wrote six chapters of a full-blown novel—the scenes and plot being laid, as I intended, in Granada. However, when I had proceeded so far, I came to the conclusion that my plan was impracticable—in a word, I have not the proper material and, indeed, could not use it if I had. Collins seems quite pleased with what I had done; but for the present I must lay it by and see if I cannot get upon some design more suited to my equipment.*

"*Since then I have been writing away at a narrative poem in rhyming pentameter couplets, and am vastly pleased with my work, that is as compared with anything I have done hitherto. I have on hand 300 lines, and when you come down at Easter will doubtless be able to read you the whole of it, completed and polished. You see I have not been idle. We must work, John, and keep our pens perpetually to paper. What plans have you? I need hardly ask, however, for the exigencies of a college education weigh on one like a kind of famine, and when I look back on it now it seems to me that a man cannot be expected to do anything original while lectures and examinations are hanging, however remotely, about his imagination. We shall be out of it all together some day, and then the working season will begin—and with old Joseph Edmund to egg us on we shall surely do something.*

"*I went to hear Matthew Arnold and was filled with an abiding sense of reverence and affection for that splendid old fellow, who looks and acts and speaks as nobly as he writes. Mr. Louis Frechette has taken offense at some of his stingless words in Montreal . . .*"

Matthew Arnold's American lecture tour, in 1883, took him to Canada. He lectured in Montreal and in

Ottawa, where he was a guest of the Marquis of Lansdowne at Rideau Hall.

The Louis Frechette incident is explained in the following extract from a letter from Matthew Arnold to Walter Arnold written in New York, February 28th, 1884:

". . . I made a speech in the two-thirds ultra-montane and one-third Orange Montreal, in which I said that the pretensions of the Catholic Church on the one hand and the Black Presbyterians on the other, hindered the fusion of French and English in America, but I looked to literature for gradually softening and opening men's minds. Some of the Catholics resented this, but the Protestants took it better by far."

The following letter, written that summer to his friend, shows Lampman still active in prose and verse writing, though harassed at times by lack of confidence and inspiration:

"The 'St. Nicholas' has returned the 'Hans Fingerhut' with no acknowledgement but their ignominious printed form. 'Tis all I expected. From this time forward I shall never lift a hand to get anything of mine published, but shall simply go on patiently amassing work of as good a quality as possible and wait for accident to do the rest.

"I have really nothing to tell you, save that I have a fine crop of radishes coming on and that I have added fifty lines or so to 'Arnulph' and am cogitating over two or three large designs for verse, which are growing in my mind. What a great assistance self-conceit is to diligent and effective writing! I have alternating periods—the period of vanity and the period of self distrust. Sometimes for weeks together I get into my head mysteriously that I have power to do something and then I can work away—write at any time—make my fingers fly like ostriches. Then comes the opposite mood, and I can do nothing. The slightest self-distrust utterly unnerves one. The only condition in which

one can write properly seems to be that of happy self-approval. I am in the barren wilderness at present. The only thing to do is to read and study myself back again.

"I have been endeavouring to think up some plan for a strictly Canadian poem, local in its incident and spirit, but cosmopolitan in form and manner. It is a hard thing to get at. I have been dreaming, however, of locating some simple story in the Niagara district, among the old farm-steads—something in accordance with the quiet toilsome life there—maybe dated forty or fifty years back in rougher times—making it sober and realistic, so to speak, in the metre of Evangeline but more like Hermann and Dorothea, or, nearer still, to the translations from a Swedish poet, Runeberg, who wrote lovely things about the peasants of Finland. I think I shall endeavour to carry this idea out."

"Hans Fingerhut's Frog Lesson," referred to above, was a prose fairy tale first published in Dr. Playter's magazine, "Man," and later in "Rouge et Noir." It was the story of a German minstrel who became so bitter that he was changed into a frog until he should have found out the meaning of the song of the stream. The result was that after much misery he again became a minstrel, and his songs were changed to happy ones. "The Song of the Stream-drops" from this story later appeared in the "Collected Poems."

From the above extracts from very personal letters it is evident that Lampman was not without inspiration and, everything considered, it was very fortunate that of all Canadian cities he should have lived in Ottawa. Toronto and Montreal were larger and less favorably situated, Quebec was quaint and picturesque, but very French; the cities of the middle west were then in their infancy, and, though the surroundings of Vancouver and Victoria are superb, they were too far from literary influences and markets. Ottawa was small enough not to crush out individuality or impose upon its citizens too much artificiality of life, and yet, as the capital of the Dominion, it contained people intellectually superior to those in most Canadian cities of its size. Moreover, the city and its surroundings were picturesque and beautiful. Situated at the junction of the Ottawa, Gatineau and Rideau rivers, it was dominated by the central mass of the towers of the Parliament buildings, built of coloured stone in early Gothic design, undoubtedly the finest public buildings in the Dominion. Lampman used to think of the city as the Florence of Canada. Just as, according to old Vasari, not even in Rome could the Florentine artists work so well as in their native city, so to Lampman Ottawa and its environs were especially conducive to artistic creation. "Perched upon its crown of rock," he said, "a certain atmosphere flows about its walls, borne upon the breath of the prevailing north-west wind, an intellectual elixir, an oxygenic essence thrown off by immeasurable tracts of pine-clad mountain and crystal lake. In this air the mind becomes conscious of a vital energy and buoyant swiftness of movement rarely experienced in a like degree elsewhere."

He had various favorite haunts, any one of which could be reached in half an hour after the office closed. Some of these were to Rockcliffe, along the Russell Road to Dow's Swamp, the Hog's Back locks, and the Experimental Farm. From all of these Lampman could obtain very fine views of the city, and this probably accounts for the repeated occurrence in his poetry of lines describing the city in the distance. (1)

---

(1) THE CITY. "The bell-tongued city with its glorious towers."
THE MEADOW. "Yon city glimmering in its smoky shroud.
SUNSET. "Cupola and pointed tower
Darken into solid blue."
ACROSS THE PEA-FIELDS. "Then the high city, murmurous with mills."
A JANUARY MORNING. ""The slender misty city towers upborne
Glimmer faint rose against the pallid blue."
WINTER UPLANDS. "The far-off city towered and roofed in blue
A tender line upon the western red."

Always a close observer of animal and plant life, he was often joined in his rambles by his friend, Dr. Fletcher, of the Experimental Farm, one of the greatest of Canadian naturalists. They knew where all the choicest flowers could be found, and it must have been after some such walk that Lampman wrote as follows:

"April and May are the months of wood flowers; June the season of blossoming in the inner recesses of the forest; August the time of perfume and colour in meadow and field. He who journeys homeward from the woods on one of these quiet, murmurous April evenings, when the light still lingers in the clear, greenish west, bears with him a handful of the tenderest and most delicate of all the flowers. Here are the hepatica, white, violet-blue or tenderest pink, plucked with last year's rusted leaves; the adder tongue drawn cool out of the moist earth, with purple-spotted leaf-blades and white, slender root-stem, curling joyously back its yellow petals under the noonday sun; the little striped blossom of the frail Spring beauty; the dicentia or squirrel corn with its pink-stemmed wreaths of tremulous creamy drops, springing from the midst of an abundance of delicate and intricate leafage; most exquisite of all, the bloodroot's clear waxen blooms, set between its half-opened irregular grey leaves. He will have also, perhaps, a bud or two just beginning to open, of the splendid white-winged trillium, or some of the blue cobosh, that mystic looking plant with its strange and dusky but very beautiful blossoms . . . When June comes we shall get the rare and beautiful lady's slippers out of the deep wet woods, and many another surprising blossom far hidden and seldom sought; but for the present let us be content with the brave little first-comers, the happy denizens of the less secluded wilderness. These, as with the races of poets, are indeed the fairest and freshest of all."

The days at the Nicholas Street cottage were among the happiest that the Lampman family ever spent together. The poet had his long-desired room to himself, where he passed happy hours in reading, verse-making and thought. Sometime during the evening he was likely to come downstairs in his quiet, nonchalant way "Well," he would say, "I've writ a pome." And the family would stop and listen as he read. Invariably they thought it fine. The Cobourg days were long since past when the little sisters had viewed with distrust their brother's embarkation upon the sea of song. But in matters of conversation he received less consideration. Mr. Lampman senior was decidedly disputatious, and the sisters were by no means dull conversationists. The poet's voice, though not loud, had a good deal of carrying power, so that in general animated conversation he could be heard overtopping the group. He loved, both at school and afterward, to get started on a congenial topic. Seldom irritable in argument, he would increase in brilliance and wit with the excitement, so that his intimate friends were often vastly amused and stimulated by a man whom the world considered quiet and aloof.

As the years went by Lampman became more and more accustomed to life in Ottawa and its uneventful routine of office work, writing, walks and chats.

He did not care for parties and avoided them whenever possible. "*A room full of whist players*," he said, "*is a spectacle to make a philosopher weep, and a progressive euchre party will turn the head of a sensible man grey in a single night.*" Most of such amusement it seemed to him was due to a hysterical desire to be on the move and the unreal laughter and meaningless conversation which accompanied it had nothing to do with real pleasure at all. "*Most of the enjoyments that we really have we find in those unregarded and unsought hours which we profess to consider the most tedious—hours of quiet and unselfish activity, when we are not thinking in the least of pleasure—hours touched with the tenderness of friendship or domestic love, with spirits kindled to a crystal flame by the earnestness of quiet and undemonstrable converse. These are the things that feed and succour the soul and redeem the melancholy of life.*"

He made, at about this time, a valued and long-loved friend in Duncan Campbell Scott, who was practically his own age and, like him, was a minister's son. Both were employed in the civil service, though Scott was already showing an ambition and aptitude which later were to give him a high place in the Department of Indian Affairs. But their most common bonds were their fondness for poetry and the open. Neither was very approachable, but their friendship warmed, and they were often to be seen together in Ottawa streets, on walks through Rockcliffe or to the Hog's Back locks, and at meetings of the Literary and Scientific Society. They stimulated each other by mutual criticism, for both were writing verse. Often they would go canoeing on the Ottawa or up the Gatineau, and they had many a pleasant outing on week-end camping trips.

One of these trips, with three other men, was undertaken on the advice of one of their number, who had discovered a beautiful spot a few miles up the Gatineau, which he recommended in everything except accommodations. When the party had proceeded there by train they found that the Irish landlord, already supplied with several guests, was even more independent and surly than they had anticipated. They had to beg for a meal and sleeping quarters. The meal was very bad, and they were hustled out of the dining-room by their inconsiderate host in the midst of a philosophic discussion. That night after each had gone to sleep in a very hard bed, they were forced to get up and re-arrange themselves at one o'clock in the morning upon the host entering and carrying off half the bedding, declaring that two blankets were too many for any one man and that they must sleep two in a bed. But next morning they forgot their troubles when they had ferried across the river and followed the winding wood roads amid the August sounds of hermit thrush and woodpecker and locust, up to a hill-top from which they looked our over rolling farms, forests and gleaming river, and there they built a cairn—an expression of the sheer enjoyment of nature and one another's society.

There were also other men beside Scott in whose comradeship Lampman found common ground, not only in fondness for nature and poetry, but in a new interest in the social problems of the day, then much under discussion.

The study of socialism in the nineteenth century developed more slowly in England than on the continent, and in Canada and in the United States later than in England. Owenism and Chartism were of the first half of the century. Charles Kingsley, in "Alton Locke" in 1849, gave expression to the ideals of Christian Socialism —an attempt to settle social problems in the spirit of Christian brotherhood. In 1862 came Ruskin's "Unto this Last," and the publication of Henry George's "Progress and Poverty" in 1879 roused radical thinking on more subjects than that of rent. The writings of Carl Marx, long popular on the continent, resulted, in England in 1881, in the formation of the Social Democratic Federation. From it William Morris and others seceded in 1885, Morris having enlarged socialistic thought to embrace art and becoming later strongly anarchistic. In 1883 the Fabian Society was established, led by such men as Sydney Webb, Sydney Olivier, Bernard Shaw, William Clarke, Graham Wallas, Hubert Bland, and E. R. Pease. Their object was to socialize British industry not by fostering sharp breaks in political systems but be educating the progressive political parties and the public to higher social ideals. They appealed especially to the cultured middle classes, and by publishing the results of their research and analysis they accomplished much.

In Ottawa at this time there was a group of men, typical of their century in intellectual curiosity but superior perhaps to most Canadians, in their serious and persistent interest in social and political problems. Some of these were W. D. Le Sueur, Rev. Mr. Walkley, A. C. Campbell, J. H. Brown, James Macoun, Wilfred Campbell, D. C. Scott, and Lampman. These met informally from time to time to discuss current problems. In addition, there was a Progressive Club which discussed Science and Religion and the many problems arising from the writings of Darwin and Huxley. No doubt Lampman was influenced somewhat by the flaming socialism of his friend, James Macoun. With A. C. Campbell, he would argue vigorously but never be quite converted by him to Henry George's views of single tax. He was said to be a Fabian, but it is doubtful if he ever identified himself very definitely with any sect. Yet the ideal end of socialism was always in his mind. He followed with interest New Zealand experiments in the control of public land sale, government operated railways and a democratic parliament. He believed that Canada had a wonderful opportunity to give the world an object lesson in enlightened social reform by adopting socialism as a form of government, but he was shrewd enough to realize that there was probably no country in the world in which it would be more difficult to convince the people of the desirability of such a step. In Canada there was no poverty as in Europe, few immigrants to spread propaganda, a preponderance of the farming class, and a vastness of country which made closely knit organization impossible. There was no discontent from a withheld suffrage, and, in a country where there had long been almost fanatical adherence to either a Liberal or Conservative party, chances for the formation of a new party were most unfavorable.

But he saw a changing order even in family life. The servant was becoming suspicious and self-assertive, and the mistress less confident of her own dignity. Only on the farms, where all the members of the household were treated as equals, were conditions anything but unpleasant and humiliating. The only solution he could see was "some co-operative plan of house-keeping and food-providing," strangely prophetic of the apartment house and delicatessen store.

The one subject on which he spoke out most bitterly and fearlessly was wealth. His college life had been somewhat restricted because of lack of money, and his income in Ottawa from the civil service and writing was pitifully small. There is no doubt, therefore, although the Lampmans better than any one else were said to know how to be happy though poor, that he had good reason for the denunciation of conditions in which the apportionment of wealth was so uneven. It seemed incredible to him that people could spend their lives in money-making for the sake of splendour or accumulation when they might be increasing and expanding the capacities of the soul in acquiring knowledge, cultivating the arts, achieving political or social reform, or practising personal benevolence. There was but one excuse for money-making—to do good. "The real enemy of mankind," he said, "is that emissary of Satan who says with the Cyclops in Euripides; 'Wealth, my little man, is the wise man's good; all other things are mere boasts and refinements of words.' "

Often for him the city is the symbol of a place where the best and finest of men's lives is crushed out, where beauty lies

"Dead in the depth of the struggle for gold"

The question, "What do poets want with gold?" gives a name to a much quoted poem, in which he says:

"Gold is but the juggling rod
Of a false usurping god,
Graven long ago in hell
With a sombre stony spell,
Working in the world forever.
Hate is not so strong to sever
Beating human heart from heart.
Soul from soul we shrink and part,
And no longer hail each other
With the ancient name of brother."

In the "Land of Pallas," that Utopia of his imagination, there was equality of land, money and labour:

"And all the earth was common, and no base contriving
Of money of coined gold was needed there or known,
But all men wrought together without greed or striving,
And all the store of all to each man was his own."

"In all their great fair cities there was neither seeking
For power of gold, nor greed of lust, nor desperate pain
Of multitudes that starve, or in hoarse anger breaking,
Beat at the doors of princes, break and fall in vain."

One of his sonnets "To a Millionaire," balances against a single fortune the broken hearts, the want and rage and hopelessness of a multitude of the down-trodden. In another, "Avarice," the amassing of a fortune so impoverishes the soul and wastes a lifetime that it leads man to

"Lock up the doors of life and break the key,
The simple heart-touch with humanity."

As Lampman was a mild socialist, so he was also something of a feminist. Since the middle of the century the question of women's rights had been widely discussed. In 1866 appeared Ruskin's "Of Queen's Gardens," and in 1869 John Stuart Mill published his "On the Subjection of

Women," in which he argued for equal rights for the sexes. In Lampman's day women had begun to make their way into the professions of law and medicine, and had taken to smoking and riding astride. Louise Michel, in France, and Emma Goldman, in America, had advocated revolutionary measures. The minority report of Blairs Committee of the United States Senate in 1889 had recommended woman suffrage, and Wyoming and New Zealand had already taken that step. There was much difference of opinion, however, and among Canadian writers none had written more forcibly against suffrage than Goldwin Smith in "Essays on Questions of the Day." But Lampman, though he never discussed the subject much, supported feminism. In his "Land of Pallas" the women "stood equal with the men." He said that no sensible man would believe that with moral and intellectual emancipation, women would sacrifice any of the grace and beauty which is their chief charm, but would gain instead in graciousness and dignity. He admitted that women were unfitted for certain occupations because of century-long lack of training, but he thought that there were no mental and few physical occupations for which they were not as equally fitted as men. "When the coming generations of women shall have been admitted to full freedom of movement and the practice of every human activity and shall have perfectly adapted themselves to the changed conditions, our children's children shall know a type of women of which we can only dream—natural queens among men, to whom they shall look up, as the Goths of old did to their Abruna women, superhumanly beautiful, superhumanly wise."

Lampman's writing and thought was usually characterized by great common sense. Most of his literary judgments have stood the test of time. He was not an extremist in socialism and feminism in days when bias was prevalent, and in some ways he anticipated modern conditions. For instance, the choice of a vocation concerned him. Success, he thought, was not the result of ability only, but of the happy choice of a life-work. Perhaps he recollected his own ventures in pedagogy, and thought how hampered, or even annulled, the usefulness of his life would have been in that profession. Too often this choice was made without regard to aptitude or inclination. He recalled a woman with a genius for the stage and opera who had grown old before her time because she had not been allowed to develop her talent. "People often discourage the development of certain talents in their children," he said, "because they consider the careers to which they lead undignified, not respectable, or dangerous to morality. In this case too, they make a mistake. There is always a much greater moral danger to be apprehended from a thwarted ambition, a native mental energy curbed and repressed, than from any action. The yearning for artistic expression in any form is a particularly dangerous one to repress."

While the Lampmans were together in the Nicholas Street cottage, their own very pleasant family life was enlivened by a few of the poet's friends, but the household had to be broken up when one sister went to New York and another, accompanied by her mother, to Germany to continue her study of the piano.

It was during their absence that Lampman met and fell in love with Maud Playter. Her father, Dr. Edward Playter of Toronto, was a friend of the family, and in his magazine "Man," Lampman's work had already appeared. She was a tall, blonde girl of delicate beauty, and so young that her father sought to restrain the romance by limiting the lover's visits. He was allowed to call only one night a week and sometimes to come to tea on Sunday. But parental rules can occasionally be evaded and even annulled, and on September 3rd, 1887, Lampman was married to his eighteen-year-old bride. His financial prospects were not very bright, for although he was nearly twenty-six his salary was painfully small, and almost none of his writing had brought him in any money; but a few days earlier one of his poems had appeared for the first time in the American "Scribner's," and he had enough more to make a good sized volume. Matrimony he undertook as he did everything else, in a mingled mood of philosophy and adventure.

The following year his wife received a small legacy, and so, without the anxiety of awaiting the publishers' decisions, they were able to print, at their own expense, quietly, but with infinite care and pride, his first book of poems, "Among the Millet," of which the dedication read:

TO MY WIFE.

Though fancy and the might of rhyme,
    That turneth like the tide,
Have borne me many a musing time,
    Belovèd, from thy side,

Ah yet, I pray thee, deem not, Sweet,
    Those hours were given in vain;
Within these covers, to thy feet
    I bring them back again.

CHAPTER VII.

"AMONG THE MILLET"

ANADIANS have always been concerned about the status of their national literature and discussion of this subject was particularly keen during the eighteen-eighties and nineties. In such debate Lampman took little part, but the names and opinions of those who did, indicate the general interest in the condition of Canadian literature which was felt in those days.

According to G. Mercer Adam, who for over 30 years was so closely identified with Canadian editing and publishing, the year 1884 saw a literary interregnum. There was an ebbing of the national spirit, an enfeebled journalism, a decrease in the book trade with England and America, an objectionable government tax on books, and an unfair copyright law. He asserted that Canadians were almost wholly taken up with bread-winning, and that in the large towns the number devoted to reading might almost be counted on the fingers. "Barry Dane" (Mrs. J. E. Logan) contended that there would be no distinctive Canadian literature because the country lacked a barbarous infancy, a mythological background, a language sprung from conflicting dialects. J. E. Collins, Lampman's friend, attributed Canadian backwardness to the fact that there were no wealthy leisure classes to foster literature, and, though there was a political union of provinces, no spiritual union existed.

By 1887, the editor of "The Week," mindful of Roberts, Phyllips, Stewart, Duvar, O'Hagan, Mrs. Harrison, and Ethelwyn Wetherald, was beginning to think that perhaps a literary renaissance was becoming more probable. In this year was published 'Seranus' Birthday Book," a representative anthology of Canadian verse with biographical notes, in which there were three quotations from Lampman and in which he is referred to as the author of "fugitive verse of high merit, mostly Swinburnian in style."

By 1889, Mr. Adam was beginning to think that the Philistine opinion, that no good could come out of a Canadian Nazareth, had obtained too long, and on January 20th of that year such thought took practical form in a meeting in Toronto of the Young Liberal Club under the presidency of Frank Yeigh. At this literary symposium, Miss Machar's "Mystic Singer" was read; "Seranus," W. D. Lighthall, Pauline Johnson, D. C. Scott, and Helen Merril contributed; and an excellent impression seems to have been made by Wilfred Campbell, who read from his own poetry.

Basil Tempest, writing in "The Week" in 1891, pointed out that, though there were no ruined castles in Canada and fewer fairies in the woods than for a European child it was foolish to say that Canadian surroundings had an unfitness for poetry. In the same publication in the following year, an author signing himself "Alchemist" offered the following suggestions: to improve the market for Canadian books through an active literary agent who would undertake publication, get up subscription lists, develop foreign markets, etc.; to induce Sir John A. Macdonald to find places for literary men in the Civil Service; and to employ Canadian rather than "foreign" professors in the universities. To this Principal Thomas Adams of Bishop's College, Lennoxville, replied that *litterateurs* had always had to endure hardships, and, objecting to the term "foreign," indicated that in his opinion the primary duty of a professor was to teach, and that national considerations were secondary.

In 1892 an effort was made in Toronto to establish a local literary salon, but the self-consciousness arising from the imposition of evening dress at the function was apparently too much for the success of the project, though Sanford Evans championed formal dress as a natural concomitant to elegance of thought and expression. Arnold Haultain, writing in "The Lake" magazine in August, 1892, following Carlyle's thesis that the healthy know not their health, suggested that it was useless to go up and down the land crying out for a production of national literature, that literature was a spontaneous thing and would find expression when the right time came, and that time was not likely to come till Canada would have "time, education, wealth and leisure, and probably vicissitudes of national fortune, wars and rumours of wars, perhaps even bloodshed and a fight for hearths and homes."

While preparing the programme for a Canadian literary evening, held at Victoria College, Toronto, on February 9th, 1894, Professor L. E. Horning, to whose interest in literature and education Canada will always be indebted, asked a number of authors to give their views on the present state and outlook for the future of Canadian literature. Charles Mair, the pioneer poet and author of the drama, "Tecumseh," replied that there had been much versifying but little poetry so far, except by Heavysedge and Roberts. J. G. Bourinot, writer on legal and historical subjects, said that Canada was hampered by colonial attitude and provincialism, yet, in spite of this and too much hasty writing, there had been a steady growth in the last fifty years. Wilfred Campbell, poet and dramatist, wrote that landscape verse had been overdone, that there was little hope for literature if it was to consist of a few polished sonnets and delicate lyrics, that false magazine standards had led to superficial verse, and that Canada was too much impressed by the neighbouring decadent American School. Duncan C. Scott, Lampman's friend and fellow poet, believed that this was a transition period, with progress discernible ahead through university influence and a growing cordiality to Canadian writing and periodicals. "Fidelis" (Miss Machar) thought the literature of the past, in view of the small population, had been under-estimated, and she sounded a note of warning against writers rushing into print, encouraged by over-patriotic praise, low standards and weak competition. J. W. Longley, the lecturer, saw literature not as something magic but simply the expression of a people, articulate when the proper time came. The imperialistic George Stewart found Canadians lacking means of expression since Canadian magazines could not compete with British and American. He did not believe that Canada must become an independent nation before it could have a literature. John Reade, of the Montreal "Gazette," found Canadian prose writers especially faulty and thought the universities might do much to improve literary style. W. D. Lighthall, prominent in Montreal legal and literary circles, saw much valuable material but little originality in Canadian poetry as yet and felt that Canadians should devote themselves to developing a school which should be distinctly national in spirit. The future depended upon organization, ideals, college teaching adapted to a growing nation, and a personal interest in Canada which should make patriotism a part of religion.

Thus there were many views, in the main, encouraging. But it was left for Goldwin Smith, one of the cleverest if least popular men of his time, to sound the depths. Said he: "No such thing as a literature in the local sense exists or is likely ever to exist." A writer in Ontario, according to him, had hardly any field outside his own province, owing to the fact that Quebec was chiefly French and that the other provinces were distant and sparsely populated. Even in Ontario with a population of little over two million there were few readers among the wealthy. Only local subjects could be sold provincially and the Copyright law almost forced publication in the United States. Moreover, people would always sell where best paid. There was no use, he concluded, to try to galvanize into life anything which had not life itself, and it was a vain attempt to try to make Toronto the "Athens of the Dominion." To this characteristic article a journalist signing himself "Canadian," replied in a more idealistic and optimistic vein that commercialism cannot last forever, that the best work of the past has been done without regard for remuneration, that it was impossible that Canadian aspirations, confidence and beauty would not produce a literature some time in the future, and that for the present, Canadian writers would value a word of encouragement so rare in Goldwin Smith.

By 1896 Archibald McMechan, the Dalhousie professor, had said that in spite of Canada being called a raw democracy with no soul above railroads and village politics, it had at least three writers who had the ideal note, Roberts, Lampman, and Parker. And at the same time Thomas O'Hagan reminded Canadians that the Chicago "Inter-Ocean" had said that Campbell's "Mother" was the best poem written in America in the last twenty years, that the Paris "Figaro" stated that many Canadian poems had been translated into French, and that the London "Spectator" ranked Lampman with Longfellow.

With the status of Canadian literature and his place in it, Lampman was never very much concerned. "The

Week" was the only Canadian magazine which took much of his verse, and no Canadian publisher would risk printing a book for him during his lifetime. Much of the criticism which appeared in Canada was inexact, since it was limited by lack of insight or biased by national pride. The reception of Lampman's work in his native land was encouraging as far as it went, but he had too broad an outlook to feel that Canada owed him a literary living or to join very heartily in any injudicious propaganda for a local literature. Yet there was probably more conscious effort to produce a Canadian literature during his time than at any other, until the present.

Moreover, that there were appreciative, though silent, readers is shown by a reminiscence, years after, by Peter McArthur, the journalist, recalling the days when Campbell, Carman, Scott, Roberts and Lampman were first winning their laurels. "To a group of young enthusiasts at the University of Toronto and in the newspaper offices," he said, "the appearance of a new poem by one of these poets was an event of the first importance. The one who first discovered the poem hurriedly called a conclave in a boarding-house somewhere in the vicinity of Huron Street, and we revelled in our find. Our best reader would read it aloud and we would go over it line by line. Those poems meant more to us than 'the glory that was Greece and the grandeur that was Rome.' Our souls vibrated to their new and native melody, and we were proud that the singers were Canadian. And now that I know more of life and have enjoyed the friendship of these poets, I know how much it would have heartened them if we had sent them a word to tell them of our hero-worship. But we were all fresh from the farms and our heroes were 'more than mortal.' I doubt if the presumption of addressing them ever entered our thoughts even in our wildest moments of enthusiasm."

It is by such unasked, non-professional appreciation that a literature is supported, and because Lampman's work appealed to the young Peter McArthurs as well as to the seasoned American critics it could afford to be judged by standards not merelv national and await a more mature and lasting evaluation.

With the publication of "Among the Millet" in 1888, Lampman at once took a definite and rather high place in the ranks of Canadian writers. His work was, of course already known through the medium of Canadian periodicals: "The Week," "Arcadia," "Canadian Illustrated News," etc., and the American "Scribner's." But a book somehow, gives dignity and definiteness of standing, and likewise carries its author's name farther afield.

Miss Lilly Barry, in reviewing the book in "The Week," said that Lampman was one of the select few to whom Canadians looked for literary independence. She spoke of the freshness in thought and phrase, the trivial touches so valuable in giving local colour, his happy descriptive power in passing from the seen to the unseen, the charming comparisons, the country peopled with a nature almost human, and the city with its varied types. She found in him none of the frequent errors, the unconscious foolish pride, the naive self-complacency one might expect in a man under thirty. "His poems, though strongly marked with his individuality, are decidedly impersonal. His soul is of the convex order. It loves to diffuse its own light and is careless about concentrating upon itself every visual ray within its focus. His love poems are delicately pure—brooding and hallowing. Though a man of active sensibility, he is supereminently a man of sense." Of narrative she thought his "Organist" the most popular. Perhaps he was lacking in exuberance, though there were touches of humour. "His sonnets show that he will not be overridden by Pegasus but leads him as he will. There is no word or a suggestion of despair in the whole book; not a drop of spleen, not a breath of sin. And yet it is quite happily free from virtuous cant or commonplace morality. It is, in a word, the product and exponent of a great soul, a gentle heart, a refined taste and a pure life. It is a book of much meaning, merit and dignity, and takes its place, as a matter of course, among the best works of our best writers."

At the same time, another reviewer, "Fidelis" (Miss Machar), was expressing a slightly less laudatory estimate of the book. She praised its imaginative power, delicacy of perception and faithfulness of description, its careful technique, its power and pathos. The title she thought not characteristic. "Winter Hues Recalled," though beautiful, seemed to lack a *raison d'etre*, to be a frame rather than a picture. "The Frogs," universally admired, she found insufficient in theme, a *tour de force* as was the much talked of "Dog" sonnet. "Between the Rapids" showed him at home in the domain of human interest. "Easter Eve" was too hopeless for a Christian subject, and the "Three Pilgrims" too harrowing to be read through. The sonnets "Music," "Sight," "Knowledge," "In November," and "Autumn Maples" were his best work.

C. M. Holmes, of Picton, wrote the following poem on the book:

AMONG THE MILLET

BY LAMPMAN.

Yes, Nature's hand is 'gainst his lips,
The secret of her finger tips
Are his! His ear is near her heart,
He hears the buds and blossoms start,
The streams awake, the loving wind,
Which stoops to coax the grass, unbind
Its old worn clasp! the Robin, too,
Who flings his songs athwart the blue,

And taunts the echoes far and near,
In reckless gladness! These appear
And take fine form from his rich soul,
He feels and knows, and scans the whole
And gathers in his dewy rhyme
The glamour of the whole springtime.

. . . .

Though Jonson was successful in writing on Shakespeare, Wordsworth on Milton, and Keats on Chapman, criticism in verse of one poet by another is a difficult matter. This became sadly apparent in the following treatment of Carman and Lampman, with a score of others, by "Clio" in the "Dominion Illustrated Monthly" for November, 1892:

"Hail Carman, in thy robe of mist,
Adorned with streaks of amethyst
Whose cut the cold logician crazes:
Hail Lampman! prone to pensive mood,
In love with nature's virginhood,
Among the Millet and the daisies.

True singers both, if for the sake
Of beauty's charm we freely make
Concessions granted Keats and Shelley;
Your dainty verses serve, at least,
To round a sentimental feast,
Divinely flavored cream and jelly."

. . . .

A critic in the London "Spectator," wisely confining himself to prose, on January 12th, 1889, published a review of "Among the Millet" which was comprehensive and favourable. The reviewer said that Lampman was not a new genius but that there was something about the combination of Canadian scenery and classical culture in his poetry which arrested the reader's attention at once. He thought his "Truth" sonnet too negative and creedless to be of value and his reference to poets as "half-god, half-brute" as too typical of the pessimism of the age. But he liked the humour in the droll photograph of the dog, and the optimism of "What do poets want with gold?" He commended the pictorial qualities of "Among the Timothy" (even though he was not quite sure what timothy was), and the Wordsworthian delight in "Winter Hues Recalled." On the human side, the "Organist" was pathetic; "Easter Eve" striking, and "An Athenian Reverie" indicative of thorough culture. "Between the Rapids" was perhaps the finest expression of human interest and scenic description, and a conclusive proof that he was capable of uttering the "true lyrical cry."

Another English critic who reviewed the book was William Sharp, in "The Academy," London, November 23rd, 1889. Canada, he said, both in history and scenery was rich in poetic material, so far best expressed in the *chansons* and *voyageur* songs of the French, yet he saw signs of a change, in the work of a number of Canadian poets, particularly Isabella Valancy Crawford, who, though unequal and intermittent, surpassed in imaginative fervour even Roberts, Lampman and Scott, and whose death was the passing of "a fair hope for Canadian literature." He saw the influence of Keats on Lampman's verse so "sensuous in sentiment, rich in colour, delicate in its harmony." He thought him unsuccessful in blank verse, and quoted lines from "An Athenian Reverie" to prove it. But whenever Lampman dealt with Nature he found him unmistakably the poet, in vivid realism, in fullness of colour. Canada, he said, had as yet produced no great poet, but he believed Lampman's to be the most finished and able verse so far.

But the most valuable friend which "Among the Millet" made for its author was William Dean Howells of "Harper's Magazine," who regarded himself almost as his discoverer. Lampman, like the Kentucky poet Cawein, seemed to Howells "always to have the right word on his lips." The word was not usually so full of colour perhaps as Cawein's, but it was sometimes of even finer meaning, and in sonnets like "The Truth" Lampman showed signs of deeper thought. In "The Frogs" he displayed "a high courage for the unhackneyed features and aspects of the great life around us." Howells quoted certain fine lines, and concluded that, though he was not a prophet by profession, he believed that even if Lampman should write no more, his fame could "only await the knowledge of work very uncommon in any time."

Later discriminating criticism of Lampman's "Among the Millet" poems were made at various times by Arthur Stringer, G. H. Unwin, and Lawrence Burpee. Mr. Stringer in the "Canadian Magazine," April, 1894, found him "less scholarly than Roberts, less imaginative than Campbell, less mysteriously melodious than Carman, less pleasing in daintiness and occasional felicity than Scott, but strong and broadest of the group in possessing most of what Landor called 'substantiality'." Though the medium through which he saw nature was a particularly white light, he could not be called a realist. For example, "the poet establishes a strong bond of sympathy between men and those dreamy pool-bubblers, the frogs. It is the poet who finds the latent beauty in what the world thoughtlessly passes over as prosaic or repulsive. Whoever before thought there was so much sentiment connected with that little, neglected, abused, serio-comic animal—the frog?"

Mr. Unwin, writing in the "University Magazine," February, 1917, discerned in "Among the Millet" various influences—of Keats in style, Arnold in thought, occasional glimpses of Wordsworth or Tennyson, but always the personality of native genius. "Among the Timothy" was reminiscent of Wordsworth's "Excursion," though Lampman carefully avoided expressing any philosophy of life other than to draw courage from nature to live rightly. Keats' methods had evidently been studied in writing "The Monk." For classical and mediæval themes Lampman was perhaps too meditative and leisurely. In the sonnets he struck a mean between the severe and ornamental styles and disproved any accusations of a carelessness sometimes said to be Canadian.

Lawrence J. Burpee, in "North American Notes and Queries," September, 1900, felt that some of the grandeur of Dante was suggested in "Easter Eve," which was also not unlike Stephen Philip's "Christ in Hades." "The Child's Music Lesson" showed how fond Lampman was of children, and in "An Athenian Reverie" it was evident that he not only knew but felt the Grecian atmosphere. "A forest pool or passing cloud," he said, referring to Lampman's personification of nature, "under his soft touch attains life and individuality."

To the modern reader of Lampman, the most evident fact about his work is that it shows few of the tendencies of the pioneer. It did not lack in flashes of his own personality, but it was backward-looking in its manners and forms. Wordsworth, Keats, Tennyson, Browning, Arnold, were its progenitors. The over-long, somewhat undramatic, sometimes sentimental narrative poems now seem unreal and ineffectual, though they were in accordance with the taste of the time. The elaborate personifications, the carefully worked out comparisons, the amassing of many details in the picture lest some feature of the landscape be missing, make some of his poetry seem heavy, verbose, prolonged. Nor did his verse always escape a moralizing too apparent to be artistic. In view of the age in which he wrote, perhaps Lampman is not entirely to be blamed for these shortcomings.

It was when he wrote out of his own heart and experience that he was at his best. The pulsing vigour of "Spring on the River," the exquisite impressionism of "Morning on the Liévre," the spiritual release of his address to the wind in "Storm," the admiration for nature in "Winter Hues Recalled," the love passion or the devotion to ideals in the sonnets, these are the real Lampman become vocal. And in the expression of this very genuine emotion there was the additional merit that his poetry was based on a careful study of the best verse forms, so that, though it was not experimental, it was, for the most part, very satisfying in workmanship, sometimes lyric often spontaneous, occasionally rising to heights almost of grandeur in phrase or line. Moreover, in poems like "The Frogs," "Heat," and "The Dog," there were indications that he was not entirely in the thrall of the conventional in treatment or viewpoint.

What had happened in the publication of "Among the Millet" was that Lampman had given expression to most of his qualities. It is true that he afterwards wrote many beautiful sonnets, felicitous studies of nature, good narrative poems, and earnest utterances of personal emotion or philosophy which displayed beauty and power. But except for certain autobiographical verses rising from later life, or the poems expressing that Utopian philosophy which concerned him more and more in his last years, there is nothing which he had not already done successfully in "Among the Millet." This volume displayed him as a varied rhymester, an adequate teller of tales, a serious thinker, a pictorial artist, and a classicist, but chiefly as an apostle of the beauty, feeling, and meaning of the Canadian scene, a title by which he will always be best and most widely known.

CHAPTER VIII.

FIRST BOSTON VISIT: 1891.

IN the late 80's Lampman became friendly with W. D. Lighthall, of Montreal, probably through the production of the latter's anthology, "Songs of the Great Dominion." The Easter of 1890 he spent with the Lighthalls in Montreal and was later their host in Ottawa. The two men had common interests in writing, and exchanged letters and work for criticism.

The vacation of that year Lampman and Scott spent on the Lower St. Lawrence, at Les Eboulements, which they reached by boat from Montreal. It was a change from the river and lake country of the interior to the farm and fishing scenes on the broad shores of the great river and the air had, instead of the fragrance of the pines, the tang of the sea. It was there that Lampman wrote one of his finest sonnets, "Sunset at Les Eboulements."

The next summer he spent his holidays with another friend and in new surroundings, for on the morning of Sunday, August 23rd, 1891, he arrived in Boston, for the first time leaving his native land. At the station he was met by E. W. Thomson, his host, and by George Iles, of Montreal and New York, writer of scientific books and subsequently donor of most of the money for the publication of the posthumous edition of Lampman's collected poems. Thomson and Lampman had been intimate for some time, but particularly since Thomson, in capacity of editor of the Toronto "Globe," had written a friendly editorial suggesting government recognition and fostering of Canadian genius by the appointment of men like Lampman to better positions in the civil service. Lampman, in return, had made efforts to place some of Thomson's stories with the editors of "Scribner's" and "Harper's," in whose magazines his poems had already appeared. They had exchanged stories and verses, and in both critical and social intercourse were a stimulus to each other. Early in the summer of 1891, Thomson had left Toronto for Boston to become editor of the "Youth's Companion," and, though Lampman was reluctant to have him go, he rejoiced in his friend's extended field of literary activity, while he himself continued in the government service where, through sheer inertia, he had written nothing for eight months. The trip, though Lampman could ill afford it and though it had to be once postponed when his wife was thrown from a carriage and badly hurt, was in every way a success and benefit. Thomson was a genial and hospitable host and introduced his guest to friends like Iles, Howe and Clayton, Mrs. Crowton, Mrs. Knowlton, Bradford Torrey, the naturalist, and Dr. Moses Coit Tyler, professor of History at Cornell. Lampman's was in no way a brilliant personality, and he was not particularly well read nor gifted with social poise, but he had an active mind, a natural refinement, and an unfailing sense of humour, and his appreciation and gift of talk made him very welcome in circles where he could be understood and loved.

That summer the residents of a tiny seaside colony on Nantucket were surprised by the arrival of two strangers, the one a tall, rugged man, the other slender, bright-eyed and rather delicate looking. They were E. W. Thomson and his friend Archibald Lampman.

Nantucket in those days was much less fashionable than now, and this particular colony was housed in a few cottages rented by an enterprising woman who served meals in one of the largest of them. It was reached by a four-mile drive from Nantucket over a road where ruts were cut deep into the sand. The cottages were unpretentious, but the huts of the fishermen added a picturesqueness to the scene and the whole spirit of the place was one of charming informality.

The two friends were long remembered by the other visitors, with whom they became quite intimate. Lampman was especially remarkable for his gayety and high spirits. Shortly after they arrived a prolonged storm swept along the Atlantic coast, keeping them virtually prisoners for three days. At meal times it was necessary to put on rubber-boots and tarpaulins and make a rush for the dining cottage. In the evenings they would all congregate in one of the cottages and there, before a blazing grate-fire, would have long talks on life and literature. Lampman and Thomson were in fine fettle and talked brilliantly, while one of the features of the evenings was Lampman's quotation of poetry from a wide range of authors, for which he had an excellent memory. He seemed to the others to have about him a Shelley-like spirituality—all soul and little body.

Yet he was quite active physically, though obviously without much reserve strength. Each day he swam in the sea. The beach there was good for a distance of about twenty feet but then suddenly dropped off to a depth of over sixty. With typical Byronic fearlessness, he paid little attention to this, until one day he swam rather far out when the sea was rough. Perhaps he was taken with a sudden weakness, perhaps he underestimated the strength of the current which that day was running strong. One of the bathers noticed that he was showing signs of distress and swam as rapidly as he could to his aid, and with some difficulty Lampman was brought to shore, where he lay exhausted for a time. It was only a passing incident in the colony, but very typical of a life-long physical weakness which could not keep up to the adventurous spirit of the man.

This almost tragic incident was succeeded by many humourous ones, for instance, the arrival of a blonde-haired actress from a stock company in Boston. She immediately became popular with the men, and Lampman and a clergyman, the Rev. Warren Partridge, began to be twitted about a sudden interest they had developed in the wild flowers of the district as soon as the actress had expressed a fondness in going for walks in search of them. There is record also of a rare and unusual service which someone thought of holding in the village church. The actress decorated the place with flowers, Mr. Partridge preached, and Thomson and Lampman helped make up the very small congregation.

While in Boston he had got lost in the crooked narrow streets, had commented on the variety of the architecture, was charmed with its ancient landmarks and its spacious Common, plunged into the congested business district at midday in a spirit of adventure, became inextricably confused over its street railway system, and in general found it the most interesting of cities.

He was fond of comparing American and Canadian types. At first the people in Boston streets seemed to him thinner and paler than those in Canada, but when he came to know some of the Bostonians he decided that that was because they were more keenly intellectual. They had a more quiet and serious bearing, a more tender kindliness and quicker sympathy. He found Boston young men less exuberant and more companionable to a thinking man, because they had reached higher levels in intellectual and moral development. Much as he admired the English or older-fashioned Canadian women, he thought the Boston women superior because their poise came not only from a consciousness of culture and position but also from a sense of the new freedom and independence which was only beginning to show itself in the younger generation of Canadians.

In spirit he found Boston carrying on the traditions of Emerson, Lowell, Hawthorne, Channing and Longfellow. Its goodness, seriousness, humanity and spirituality impressed him so much that he thought it likely that the new social reforms which seemed to him imminent might originate there, just as the anti-slavery movement had forty years before. He was told that some of the wealthiest people lived and dressed in almost Spartan simplicity, and he thought it a fine example to set for New York and other cities where the display of wealth and indulgence in luxury were ostentatious enough to be dangerous to society.

It is possible that the following poem, which appeared in the "Arcadia Magazine," May 2nd, 1892, arose from the experiences of the Boston visit:

IN THE CITY.

I wandered in a city great and old,
At morn, and noon, and when the evening fell,
And round my spirit gathered like a spell,
Its splendour and its tumult and its gold,
The mysteries and the memories of its years,
Its victors and fair women, all the life,
The joy, the power, the passion and the strife,
Its sighs of hand-locked lovers, and its tears,
And whereso in that mighty city, free
And with clear eyes and eager heart I trod,
My thought became a passion high and strong,
And all the spirit of humanity,
Soft as a child and potent as a god,
Drew near to me, and wrapped me like a song.

After Lampman's return to Ottawa, he began to write with renewed vigour and took up again the Biblical story of "David and Abigail," a long dialogue in blank verse which he had begun years before. It now seemed to him very immature, and he began reworking it with considerable misgiving, but he had a disposition to finish anything he undertook, and he was not sure that it was entirely bad. With characteristic whimsicality he would refer to it as his white elephant, his Biblical fraud, and assure himself that if he could once get it finished he would turn to something more promising. The Autumn of '91 was a busy one. Particularly short of money, he assaulted the magazines with manuscript and was encouraged by sales to "Scribner's" and others. In a few months he hoped to have enough poems for another small book, for by the end of November he had almost finished "David and Abigail," and had written half a dozen short poems, two or three sonnets and a few nature descriptions. He read a good deal too, and experienced a new interest in Charles Reade's novels, particularly "Peg Woffington" and "Christie Johnstone," which stood very well what he considered a great test, the faithful presentation of women. From Reade he turned to Lewes' "History of Philosophy," because he professed he was weary of being ignorant about such things—an ignorance of which he became conscious no doubt in some conversation during his Boston visit. Bradford Torrey had sent him his "Rambler's Lease," and in it he found knowledge, sympathy and genial fancy. To the work of Torrey and Burroughs he was drawn instinctively.

His Boston friends presently expressed their appreciation in a practical way by taking steps to have him better his position. They talked of his leaving Canada, and Dr. Tyler thought he might get him an assistant professorship at Cornell. It was pleasant to think that he had found congenial, kindred spirits across the border, and, in spite of talk of "Canada for the Canadians," it did seem as though they were appreciated less at home than abroad. There was, therefore, a good deal of planning in the Lampman household, for the poet's wife was as eager as he for removal to an American university town.

In the office the routine of work continued until a Government, anxious to impress the country with its economical administration, began to make reforms in the civil service. They proposed to prohibit the franking of letters, lengthen office hours, forbid men going home to lunch at noon, and make leave of absence difficult. These were the main features which made life in the service tolerable for Lampman, and he longed either to leave it or else have enough knowledge of political history and practice in political writing to expose with his pen what he considered unfair political dealing. Some of the most extravagant and bitter things he ever wrote were against governmental insincerity. The influx of party politicians when Parliament assembled filled him with derision. Certain of them made him regret "the falsity of the old theological fable of hell-fire." He said that whenever he saw them prowling around like blood-suckers and bunco-men his mind reverted with love and tenderness to one of the most illustrious of English heroes—Guy Fawkes. A man capable of the luminous idea of blowing up a whole building full of parliamentarians, including their ridiculous and vexatious old king, was worthy, he declared, of canonization, and he wrote to his friend Thomson that if any fragments of cabinet ministers should descend into Temple Place he would know what had happened. At the same time he would have been glad to accept, through the assistance of his friend or others, a better position in the service—not a pompous one, but some quiet office where he could work faithfully, without much notice, but with more time for composition. He was interested in leisure rather than salary, for he believed that he could add a good deal to his income by writing. He felt he could do critical articles for the magazines. He had plenty of ideas but lacked background. An article on Matthew Arnold seemed to him a good beginning. Yet the office work dulled the sharpness of his mind and family responsibilities were increasing, for on January 11th, 1892, Natalie, his first child, was born.

In watching the antics and development of his child, he found a new and constant pleasure. Her droll seriousness amused him. He liked to discuss her with his neighbours, young couples who had babies of similar age and propensities, and the fond parents exchanged humorous and felicitous comparisons, till, he declared, an atmosphere of parental happiness pervaded the whole neighbourhood.

One of his neighbors was the poet William Wilfred Campbell. Lampman's first impression of him did not inspire confidence, but his regard increased as they grew to know one another better. Campbell's erratic and somewhat slovenly mind was always surprising people by unexpected and seemingly accidental flashes of brilliance just as his vigorous personality was continually thrilling and offending them by turns. He was then living in Ottawa on the pay of a temporary clerk at $1.50 a day, and it was largely for financial reasons that Lampman and Duncan Campbell Scott at this time joined him in writing weekly articles for the Toronto "Globe" in a column which they called "At the Mermaid Inn."

CHAPTER IX.

"AT THE MERMAID INN."

THE Toronto "Globe" of the early nineties was the principal newspaper of Ontario and the chief Liberal organ for the Dominion. It was published on week-days as an eight-page daily, which sold for three cents a copy and had a circulation of about 20,000 copies. Outstanding world news and much that was of purely local interest filled its columns. The general tone, except in the case of highly partisan politics was definitely dignified, and for the most part there was no sensationalism. The advertisements included those for suits of clothes at $5.00, $7.50 and $10.00; cures for the gout; settlers' special trains to British Columbia; the performance of Edmund Keane in "Richelieu" at the Grand Opera House; Allan Line sailings from Halifax to Liverpool at $20.00 steerage, and Paderewski's first appearance in Toronto. On Fridays there was a department headed "Literary Notes," consisting of brief and rather perfunctory and dull reviews of a great variety of books. The humour was of the most slapstick variety, conveyed to the apparently none too subtle readers by means of self-explanatory drawings, the progenitors perhaps, of the modern comic strip. Sometimes the rather obvious jokes were illustrated by Dickensian drawings reminiscent of "Punch." There was an interesting column of correspondence, for "Globe" readers took life and themselves seriously and frequently composed impassioned letters to the paper on current topics, largely political and religious. The warfare over Sunday street cars and the opening of the World's Fair on Sunday gave rise to many heated communications. There was also discussion of the Copyright Act and the designing of a Canadian flag. Certainly the nineties was a controversial decade.

Once a week, on Saturdays, the "Globe" expanded to its full dimensions of twenty pages with a circulation that passed 40,000. This included an enthusiastically advertised section dealing with the history of local institutions, personages, or celebrations, illustrated with drawings by W. Thomson. These excellent pen and ink sketches ceased with the introduction of the photogravure process, and the paper launched upon a sort of pictorial tour of Ontario, in which each issue was devoted to some one city or town, with pictures of its streets, business places, homes and prominent citizens. The "Globe" was by no means unprogressive. It sent a special woman representative to the World's Fair; it published serially W. D. Howell's "Quality of Mercy" and "The American Claimant," by Mark Twain; and it began a purely literary column called "At the Mermaid Inn."

In September, 1890, the late Sir John Willison had become editor of the paper. As a Huron County youth without journalistic experience but with talent and ambition, he had earlier attracted the attention of the "Globe" editor, J. Gordon Brown, but, as no position was then vacant on the staff, he served a somewhat unlucrative apprenticeship on the London "Advertiser." Coming from it to the "Globe" in 1883, he wrote articles on current topics signed "Observer," and presently was made "Globe" representative in the press gallery at Ottawa, of which he became president in 1890. While in Ottawa he had come to know Wilfred Campbell, Duncan Scott and Lampman.

Campbell had not been happy as a rector, and when opportunity offered had taken a position in the civil service. "I gave up," he said, "$1,200 a year and a rectory to live a richer life at $500 a year." It is true that living conditions in those days were very different from now, with living simpler, and food, rents and clothing cheaper, but $500 a year was too little even for a poet, and it became necessary for Campbell to add to his income. At this juncture Sir John Willison appeared with the suggestion of a weekly literary column to be written by Campbell, Scott and Lampman at the rate of three dollars per week each. They were to have *carte blanche* as to the quantity and subject of their writing, and the monthly editorship of the column was to pass from one to another in succession. All material was to be ready by Thursday, when it was read and forwarded to the "Globe" to appear in the Saturday issue, each article signed with the writer's initials.

As a result of this arrangement, the Saturday "Globe" of February 6th, 1892, for the first time contained the column entitled "At the Mermaid Inn." The title was a particularly happy one, for it suggested immediately to any readers with literary interests the old Mermaid Tavern on Broad Street in London, where Sir Walter Raleigh was credited with founding the famous club whose members included Jonson, Beaumont, Fletcher, Selden, Carew. and, perhaps, Shakespeare; the conviviality of which Keats in a later generation declared equal to anything that might be experienced by its members in Elysium.

The second appearance of the column, on February 13th, had the further distinction of the following "quotation" at its head.

Sir Roger: "What have we here?"

Giles: "There is everything under the sun set down

with some show of reason; they run atilt at the world, and treat man and manner as familiar as an old hat."

Sir Roger: "Think you they protest too much? I like a matter disposed of bravely, but . . . "

Giles: "Methinks they have a genial tongue. Will you hear them?"

Sir Roger: "Well, an't be not too long, I'll have some sack, and you read on."

Though an impromptu invention of Scott's, this apt heading sounded Elizabethan and erudite. It indicated also that the spokesmen were to deal with a great variety of topics, and there was a pleasant suggestion of whimsical humour which showed that they did not mean always to be taken too seriously. Some four months later the quotation was dropped from the column, but the same fine flavour of genial literary *causerie* remained until the end.

Subsequent issues of the "Globe" contained a small advertisement now and then calling attention to its column written by three of Canada's outstanding *litterateurs*. It had begun by being named in type of very modest size, but before it was discontinued it was headed in fancy lettering, and in some issues was topped with a drawing of a very bare room with several figures chatting over their pipes.

The first column in variety, character and subject was typical of what was to follow. Campbell wrote a book review and inveighed against wealth. Scott also reviewed a book, took some exception to Swinburne's praise of Victor Hugo, and in discussing Canadian verse advocated a viewpoint which should be peculiarly Canadian. Lampman contributed four pieces of varying length to this issue. One was on the German Emperor's lack of humour; another dealt with a book on the Paris morgue and prisons; a third mentioned Howell's transference from "Harper's" to the "Cosmopolitan;" and the fourth discussed the best seasons of the year for writing.

But the literary venture thus begun so quietly, though auspiciously, at the outset narrowly escaped editorial extinction on account of the fluent but unguarded pen of Campbell. On February 27th, the column contained an article by him on Mythology, in the course of which he referred to the early Old Testament and the Story of the Cross as "mythical." This, in a paper supported by highly orthodox readers, was a decided *faux pas*, and the canny management, without waiting for a letter from some "Indignant Reader," hastened in the next issue to express itself in no very uncertain terms in an editorial in which the writer said that only the pressure of work had prevented him reading the manuscript, and that it was a matter of great regret that any such religious views had found a place in the columns of the "Globe." To this Campbell replied in an open letter that he had had no idea of attacking Christianity but merely had reference to the history of the cross (now printed with small "c") in ancient nature religions as being mythic in origin. Nothing further came of the incident in the paper, but it would not be surprising if Sir John entertained a passing doubt as to the wisdom of his journalistic experiment, and if in the future the Ottawa manuscript was given a more careful proof-reading.

Book reviews and literary criticism comprised the bulk of the column, but all the contributors aired their views upon current topics or pet foibles. Scott wrote on such diverse subjects as Paul Peel's death, hypnotism, the sea-serpent, and skating. Campbell on the Monks of Oka, aristocracy, hymns, and the woods in winter. Lampman on Bismark, book duties, geniuses, the servant question, church-going, and nature descriptions.

There was humour also in the column. For instance,

following the report that a Viennese professor, having learned the language of apes, had set out for Africa, Lampman hoped that he would be cautious in interviewing some of them. "An interchange of sentiments with an impulsive and able-bodied gorilla, for instance, would call for a degree of delicate diplomatic skill not at the disposal of every man." On another occasion he gave a mock heroic description of the battles of Thomas, one of the cats of which he was fond. "Like the allied armies who were so often beaten by Napoleon, he acquired the art of war. The battle shout has now no longer any terrors for him, and his wounds are all in front. Indeed, I regret to say that his ears are beginning to assume the appearance of the tattered battle flags so often noticeable in elderly and experienced tom-cats."

Somewhat in the same vein is his account of an imaginary friend, "a sonneteer," who supposedly submits the sonnet "Falling Asleep" to him for criticism. Lampman pretends to object that the subject is unsuitable in smallness and homeliness. But the "sonneteer," who is of course, himself, replies that that only makes the poem the more impressive, and to Lampman's increasing disdain he recites:

REALITY.

I stand at noon upon the heated flags
At the bleached crossing of two streets, and dream
With brain scarce conscious, now the hurrying stream
Of noonday passengers is done. Two hags
Stand at an open doorway piled with bags
And jabber hideously. Just at their feet
A small, half-naked child screams in the street,
A blind man yonder, a mere bunch of rags,
Keeps the scant shadow of the eaves, and scowls,
Counting his coppers. Through the open glare
Thunders an empty wagon, from whose trail
A lean dog shoots into the startled square,
Wildly revolves and soothes his hapless tail,
Piercing the noon with intermittent howls.

But to Campbell, writing in the "Mermaid Inn," undoubtedly goes the palm for poetic burlesque. His criticism of the poem "Red Top and Radishes," by John Pensive Bangs in the "Great Too-Too Magazine" is directed against a school of poetry so akin to Lampman's as to be not quite comfortable. Campbell's ridiculing imitation is as follows:

AT EVEN.

I sit me moanless in the sombre fields,
The cows come with large udders down the dusk,
One cudless, the other chewing of a husk,
Her eye askance, for that athwart her heels,
Flea-haunted and rib-cavernous, there steals
The yelping farm-dog. An old hen sits
And blinks her eyes. (Now I must rack my wits
To find a rhyme, while all this landscape reels.)

Yes! I forgot the sky. The stars are out,
There being no clouds; and then the pensive maid!
Of course she comes with tin-pail up the lane.
Mosquitos hum and June bugs are about.
(That line hath 'quality' of loftiest grade.)
And I have eased my soul of its sweet pain.

Of the three writers of book reviews for the "Mermaid Inn" column Lampman wrote the most and Campbell the least, but for some reason to Scott seem to have fallen the most important books. Lampman thought the humour of Barry Pain's "In a Canadian Canoe" sometimes forced. He did not like A. T. Stead's modern version of the Bible. "One might as well," he said, "have Homer by Will Carlton or Martin Farquhar Tupper as the Bible by a modern newspaperman." Robert Louis Stevenson he considered a good artist but a poor dramatist. "The Wrecker" displayed a continued "diabolical taste for bloodshed," but he appreciated the fact that Stevenson never undertakes what he cannot do, and "knows how many strokes go to the picture."

Bradford Torrey published, within a short interval, two nature books, "A Rambler's Lease" and "The Footpath Way," both of which Lampman praised unreservedly. The author of the first, he said, was an ornithologist not of the intellect only but of the heart. In reviewing the second he found him "a finer and more suggestive thinker than Burroughs, and more pleasing, if less brilliant one than Thoreau." "He is not only a most minute and patient observer after the persistent modern manner of the habits of plants and birds, but also a literary artist who possesses you with his simplicity sweetness and charm, a poet philosopher, swift to perceive and reveal the parable in every commonest operation of nature, and a humorist of that tenderly reflective sort whose jesting—if it is not too rude a word for anything so delicate—leaves the mind in a gentle and genial sunshine." Such a writer, Lampman believed, opens to his readers pleasurable vistas which place him above the poets. Much of what he said of Torrey might, indeed, have been said of himself. As patient observers writing with thoughtful intent, they had much in common.

The dozen or so books of verse which fell to Lampman's lot as a reviewer during the continuance of the column did not contain many memorable names. Some of the writers were of purely local interest. He had a kind word for George Martin's Keatsian poem, "To My Canary Bird"; he appreciated "The Lost Island" and "Nestorius" by E. T. Fletcher, a Crown Lands Department official aged 70, who wrote "without caring whether the public buy his photograph or the reviewers blow all their penny whistles in his praise"; he found in George Frederick Scott's "In Via Mortis" visions of the dead in their hidden land in a manner typical of all indigenous northern poetry; and in Arnold Haultain's "Versicule" evidences of a pure and sensitive soul whose thought, however, was generally better than his workmanship, but whose sonnet, "Beauty," had "genuine fervour, abundant fancy and many pleasant lines." Similarly, J. F. Herbin's "The Marshland" seemed to him, though not unblemished, yet having "the tone of one who loves beauty, and loves her purely and honestly." He quoted E. W. Thomson's "The Song Sparrow," but thought he meant the vesper sparrow instead. He found J. H. Brown's "Poems, Lyrical and Dramatic" sweet, speculative and of excellent workmanship. A patriotic poem by Chas. G. D. Roberts seemed to him vigorous, though somewhat forced. But to Edgar Fawcett fell the fullest measure of criticism, thus: "His talent—brilliant, ingenious, productive but artificial, overstrained and devoid of tenderness—has developed naturally in the eager and heated air of a vast city, in the midst of its awful material splendour and its spiritual *ennui*, its perpetual and complex exhibition of all the extremities of human passion and the vicissitudes of human destiny. His work is that of a man from whose soul every simple and child-like influence has been eliminated, who is driven by weariness of every ordinary emotion or natural image to find his material in the fantastic and intensely far-fetched. The imagery of Mr. Fawcett's poetry is often of the most tremendous character, but the effect upon the imagination is that of lurid unreality; it astonishes, but very soon surfeits the reader. Nevertheless, some of his pieces are so remarkable for fantastic invention and a certain sensuous verbal exquisiteness of presentation that they must be classed with the most interesting products of American genius." Lampman's prejudice against city life is interesting in view of the fact that some have thought his art would have developed better under urban conditions.

Lampman and his friends were interested readers of the magazines, both American and Canadian, and frequently reviewed them as a whole or in part; Lampman perhaps more than the others. From time to time he mentioned, "The Fortnightly Review," "The Contemporary Review," "Harper's" and "Scribner's." "The Youth's Companion" he regarded as an interesting achievement in estimating the requirements of American family life even though some considered it the reduction of the commonplace to an art. Like all Canadian writers of the time, he felt the need of a purely Canadian magazine which would encourage native writers and foster national ideals. It was especially difficult for Canadian writers of verse to publish in American magazines. Yet, in spite of this, more than seventy of Lampman's poems appeared in magazines published in the United States.

"When the intellect of a nation," he said, "first becomes conscious of the beauty and mystery of the life around it, that consciousness has in it a religious quality which utters itself most fitly in poetry." Hence most Canadian writers were poets and their only market was four or five American magazines, printing comparatively little verse. How splendid, he thought, if a half dozen wealthy men would found a magazine. He regarded the "Arcadia" as a vigorously edited magazine with a distinctly anti-humbug attitude. "The Lake" was still new; "The Week," always on high quality, had improved; The "Globe's" Saturday issue was not unimportant. Only the "Dominion Illustrated Monthly" came in for blame as a jejune and provincial effort, which he thought, should drop pictures and football and not be encouraged simply because it was Canadian.

Meanwhile, as reviewers of books and magazines, Scott and Campbell had been busy. Scott praised Meredith's "Harry Richmond" and deplored a pirated edition of "Diana of the Crossways," mentioned Philip Bourke Marston's verse, spent some pains on Gottschalk's "Notes of a Pianist," disliked Lord Lytton's "Glenaveril", quoted appreciatively from Arthur Henry Clough, and William Morris' "Poems by the Way", and disparaged Amélie Rive's play, "Edgar and Athelwold." Kipling he found vigorous but odorous of blood and fire, and W. E. Henley seemed to require too much interpretation, and to lack philosophic depth and that beauty without which sordiness is a mistake. On two occasions Scott praised Harriet Monroe's poetry, especially her sonnets. Aldrich he called "America's most artistic poet." As for the magazines, when in 1893 Joseph Gould's "Arcadia" failed after a few months' publication, Scott pointed out that since artistic circles were restricted even in the cities and in Canada did not exist in the country at all, Canadians were indebted to its editor for the experiment, even though an apparent failure.

As a reviewer Campbell displayed his characteristic vigour of opinion and expression. In contemporary poetry he praised the sincerity of Riley, thought J. H. Brown insufficiently recognized, and found fault with Lighthall's "Songs of the Great Dominion" as an anthology which excluded all poetry not of topical interest. He defended the morality in Thomas Hardy's "Tess," and disliked the happy ending in Barrie's "Little Minister." He mentioned "Essays from Reviews" by Dr. George Stewart and "Over Sea" essays by J. E. Wetherell. Miss A. M. Machar's "Roland Græme, Knight" seemed to him sensible but lacking in genius, and in Miss Mary E. Wilkins, author of "A New England Nun, and other Stories" he found a writer who brought out the repressed sentiment of New England but failed to make psychogically convincing the union of a refined woman with a brutal man. He entertained special grudges against unearned literary prominence and inexpert or insincere reviewing. He agreed with W. Blackburn Harte in "In a Corner at Dodsley's" that literary fame is often gained as a politician gains power, and he attacked the English *Athenæum* for insularity in a too brief note on the death of George W. Curtis. A writer in the "English Review" for referring to Aldrich's "Queen of Sheba" as "no better than the author's other poems," when it was prose, was the recipient of his scorn. He greeted the initial appearance of "The Lake" magazine with advice not to copy American magazines and not to limit an author's space, and in the first number of Mr. Mowat's "The Canadian Magazine" he praised an article on the stage by Hector Charlesworth.

This great variety of subjects arising from the informal organization of "At the Mermaid Inn," no doubt appealed to many readers. Probably some of the writing was somewhat extempore; but it was all characterized by good style and vigorous thinking. Scott was perhaps the most conservative and Campbell the most brilliant and erratic. In it, Lampman showed himself a thinker on many diverse topics, a discriminating literary critic, and a writer whose taste and prose style is well illustrated in the following selection:

"*If a man were to be exiled to some inaccessible island or cast into prison and given the choice of half a dozen books which he might carry with him to be his solace and support, which books do you think he would choose? No doubt every man much given to reading and thought has amused his fancy at some time or another with some such speculation as this. If it were my case, I should choose the Bible, the poems of Homer, the plays of Shakespeare, the poems of Wordsworth, the autobiography of Goethe, and the Don Quixote of Cervantes; the Bible as the most fruitful expression of the religious and prophetic spirit; the Iliad and*

Odyssey of Homer as the most perfect example of human passion and human effort presented in the clearest simplicity of beauty; the plays of Shakespeare as the picture of human life made for us by the world's highest union of intellect, heart and imagination; the poems of Wordsworth as the noblest presentment of the influence exerted upon the soul by the beauty and grandeur of outward nature; the autobiography of Goethe as the record of the development of an insatiable and most vital mind uniting the artistic and scientific spirits each in an extraordinary degree; and the Don Quixote of Cervantes as the world's book of the sweetest and most human humour. From these six books a man might draw sufficient strength, knowledge, inspiration, delight and humanity to last a life-time and leave him with his soul fitted for eternity with all its chambers draped and furnished, and all its windows open."

CHAPTER X.

LAMPMAN AS A LITERARY CRITIC.

HILE Lampman was in no sense a disciple or imitator, it would be useless to ignore the fact that he gained much from books, that they were one of his few sources of inspiration and that his thoughts about other writers and their work played a large part in the shaping of his own poetry. Fortunately, "At the Mermaid Inn" and various unpublished essays on poetry, furnish material for some estimate of him as a literary critic.

Although he was more influenced by English than American writers, he took a great interest in contemporary and earlier American literature with which he kept in touch through books and magazines. Probably the most talked of and stimulating force in American literature during Lampman's lifetime was Whitman. He had read this poet and discussed him at college, and had even mentioned him in the Orangeville letters into which literature seldom crept. In 1892 Theodore Watts had written an article in the "Athenæum" in which he said that though sometimes sublime, Whitman was obscure indecent, ungrammatical, a poseur as the noble savage, and in England would have been run in. The "Saturday Review" had dismissed his political, social and moral ideas as infantile. With these in mind, Lampman himself said, "In truth, it may be said that personality enters into the quality of Whitman's work more prominently than in the case of any other writer. It is his personality that so keenly attracts and repels, and there will always be a class of gentle and delicate minds whom, however willing they may be to recognize the frequent beauties and grandeurs in Whitman's work, his brawny egotism and raw aggressive force will instinctively repluse. The old world will acknowledge his power in theory and at a distance, but it will approach him with a shrug and a shudder." Lampman strove to keep his own poetry impersonal, and his restraint presents a contrast to that shouting in verse which is so Whitmanesque. In this he was unlike Campbell, who said with one of his flashes of terse criticism: "Emerson was universal in intellect but New England in local characteristics; Lowell voiced the sentiments of the cultured few regarding the Republic; Longfellow was essentially the laureate of the home; but Whitman in his individualism, his intense enjoyment of life, his interest in the nation and his sympathy, mirrored the American people for a quarter of a century as Dante did the Italy of the Middle Ages."

At the head of contemporary American poetry Lampman put Aldrich and Riley. According to him, the former with his idealism, his gift for beautiful phrase-making appealed to the cultured few; the latter standing at the opposite pole, found his power in touching some homely, popular chord which, with an added wit and whimsical cleverness, gained him a wider, if less discriminating public.

For Emerson he had nothing but praise. Not even his own musical sense of prosody made him object to the stilted style of a man whom Campbell called a mere "rhyming philosopher." Lampman would not even allow that Emerson was obscure, simply that his close-packed sentences required a more attentive reading, and he pointed out how admirable Emerson's essays were for piecemeal reading, since one could open them anywhere and take up the thread of some inspiring current of thought. Like his own humble-bee, Emerson was continually voyaging and stowing away his thoughts with little regard for their form. Though of New England austerity, he had a warm sympathy breaking through like sunshine on a cool and cloudy day. "Emerson was in the fullest sense a nature poet," said Lampman, "He identified himself with nature. He was not so persistent and hardy a roamer of the forest and lake as Thoreau, but his faculty of penetrating into the moods and methods of nature was as fine as his. He is drawn to nature because in the energies of his own soul he is aware of a kinship to the forces of nature, and feels with an elemental joy as if it were a part of himself, the eternal movement of life."

Another American whom Lampman liked was Henry James. To be sure, he said, one may object to the somewhat unimaginative hardness of details which James piles up in such pitiless quantity about his characters, to the sudden transitions in narrative, to the too finely drawn subtlety of many of the character sketches that "make us feel as if we were moving over a floor covered with delicate pottery in a dimly lighted room. One may feel the narrative irrelevant to the deeper meanings of life, and little more than psychological treatises cast into dramatic form. And yet, when the book is finished, the characters will remain because they are chiselled upon the mind by a thousand strokes of artistry and skill."

Upon the subject of sonnet writing he might reasonably be expected to speak with some authority in view of his own study and success in that form of verse. His general criticism of American sonnets of the time was that they were too studied and too clever, for of all forms of writing he regarded the sonnet as requiring the greatest simplicity. He considered Longfellow the greatest American sonneteer and his "Nature," "Sound of the Sea," "Milton," "Tides" and "Chimes" lacking only in ruggedness. Edgar Fawcett's were "the cleverest, the strongest, the most ingenious and the least touching." Edgar Allan Poe came nearest to writing the grand sonnet of this continent in "Silence." Bryant nearly succeeded in "October," and so did Lowell in some of his sonnets addressed to persons. Aldrich in his able and grandly sounding sonnets seemed to err on the side of cleverness and seldom showed "the patient ear and majestic self-restraint of the true sonneteer." Sidney Lanier's sank under the weight of their intricate imagery; Riley's were exquisite in impish cleverness and dainty whimsical beauty; Gilder's, especially "The Life-mask of Abraham Lincoln" came very near the ideal. Of American women writers, Emma Lazarus' "Success" and "The Venus of the Louvre" bit keenly into his memory, and among Canadians Charles G. D. Roberts had written at least one sonnet of high order in "Reckoning." Thus, for Lampman, sonnet writing necessitated high idealism, care rather than cleverness, an accurate ear, and emotion powerful though restrained. Certainly he showed himself a keen student of sonnet writing in America.

His interest in American literature was partly due, of course, to the sense of isolation which he had as a Canadian writer, dependent solely upon a few friends, himself and nature, and lacking that lively and frequent literary intercourse which is the privilege of those who live in a great metropolis. He felt that the human mind is often like a plant which becomes fecund only when associated with others. To supply this need he had his friends, two trips to American literary centres, a limited correspondence, and whatever time he could get for reading.

Lampman's standards of literary criticism both for himself and others were very high. He often urged that writers should not be overpraised on patriotic or other grounds. J. E. Collins he always regarded as a keen and constructive critic, as well as a personal literary father. Most work in Canadian periodicals, except "The Week," suffered from being either ignored or over-praised. "The young writer must remember," he said, "that he must 'scorn delights and live laborious days', that he must apply himself to intense study, to unremitting observation, to perpetual practice, if he would win fame that is worth the having."

In his fellow countryman Bliss Carman he recognized an artistic and original talent. "His poems are suffused with a new and peculiar and most beautiful imaginative spirit, a spirit which is that of our own northern land, developed in the atmosphere of the Norse, with tinges of Indian legend." He admitted Carman's obscurity, but pointed out that it was self-imposed, since that poet did not aim at clear-cut images but preferred instead to "steep his readers' imagination in splendid moods through the agency of magnificent metrical effects and a vast and mysterious imagery created under the presence of beauty."

In Charles G. D. Roberts also he saw a writer with an individual touch. He praised his phrase-making, his "vivid and luxurious delight in splendid landscape and the richness of his gift as a word-painter." His diction he found "at times a little heavy in its movement and wanting in flexibility" but having "always the charm of an exceedingly broad and full-voweled flow, with a sort of determined strenuousness of accent." Lampman was neither jealous nor unpatriotic, but he realized that an art is not necessarily good because it is national.

It has no doubt been remarked that with his contemporaries writing patriotic verse, and in view of his own early interest in patriotic, not to say warlike poetry, Lampman gave no expression in his work to national or imperialistic sentiments. Of his sincere love for Canada there is no question, but he was too broad-minded to be biased by an over-distinct racial prejudice. He felt that Canadians could not be expected to have the same intense loyalty as Englishmen, because they had in comparison so little background of race history and were, indeed, not even a homogeneous people but rather the material of which a nation is to be made. The United States had had its Civil War to help create a national tradition. As for Canada, he said, "we shall not know what national consciousness and patriotism are until something like that happens to us. If it ever comes to a question with each one of us of either sneaking off into a corner and playing the coward, or else going forth sternly for pride and honour's sake, if not for love, to risk our blood for this land's unity of independence, then in a little while we shall learn what patriotism is. The brave among us shall make it possible for our descendents to be patriotic in true sense, and not till then." [1]

Writing in 1892 on the subject of French and German war songs, he said: "When the next war shall arise, its thunder will be terrible upon the Rhine. Modern France is the France of the Revolution, and the very soul of the revolution pulses in the *Marseillaise*, a spirit wild, daring, and titanic. It is the most tremendous call to battle that ever sprang to the lips of man. Its note is inspired, fierce, and aggressive. But, like the mighty fervour that gave it birth, its passion is too high to be maintained. It represents the charge, the first splendid fury of the attack; it

---

[1] Nineteen members of the Lampman family (including the poet's son) served in the Great War.

does not fit so well the hour of uncertainty, of dogged defence, still less of miserable defeat."

Canada has always been at a disadvantage in her geographical proximity to the United States. It is true that there have been certain benefits in inspiration and intercourse with a country of greater population, wealth and artistic development, but competition has been one sided, and easy access to a country which presents greater advantages has long been a temptation to young Canadians. Nor is this condition due to any lack of appreciation on the part of Canada nor lack of patriotism among her young people. It is simply the inevitable result of economic conditions which only time can rectify, through the increased wealth, population and opportunities which will eventually be developed in Canada. Such a situation has been felt so long that it was nothing new in Lampman's day, and he once enumerated as expatriated Canadians Edward Blake, orator; Grant Allen, man of letters; Sir Gilbert Parker, novelist; Sara Jeanette Duncan, journalist; Dr. Schurman, president at Cornell; Erastus Wiman, financier; E. W. Thomson, writer; Bliss Carman, poet, and W. Blackburn Harte, journalist. He took these evidences of emigration very philosophically. "Let us find no fault with them on that account," he said; "they probably bring more honour to their own country in the fields which they have chosen than they would if they had remained at home. Here their energies might have withered away in petty and fruitless occupations and their talent have evaporated in the thin sluggishness of a colonial atmosphere." Is there more in this than appears on the surface, an autobiographical regret between the lines?

It is a fascinating, if futile, occupation to consider what would have happened if Lampman had also burned his bridges and, giving up the safe and meagre income in the civil service, sought a purely literary career outside Canada. Bernard Muddiman in the "Queen's Quarterly" of January and March, 1915, thinks it would have led to the liberation of the poet's powers and made him a greater force in literature. It is a fanciful picture he paints; Lampman, the quiet ascetic, has become fired with a fervour akin to Shelley's. No longer are there pallid and meticulous poems springing from solitary communings with nature, but instead, trumpet calls, a message for humanity born of an unrestrained life in Bohemian quarters of continental cities. Muddiman believes that the environment of respectable Ontario deprived Lampman of what was needed to set his talents free, that he had none of the joy of a wayfaring life, no great passion, no continental night life, no "spinal sensualities nor the Sufistic paradise of Keats."

No one can say definitely what another would have been under changed circumstances, but to those who knew Lampman best it would seem that his character was of the kind that lives out its inner life only half dependent upon its surroundings. It is easier to think that Paris would have cut him off so completely from nature, have presented such extremes in human nature, have intensified his natural melancholy so as to have blighted rather than vitalized his work and, like Synge, he would have had eventually to return to the country, the real source of his best inspirations. It is true that shortly before Lampman died he said he wished he could have seen life more fully in his twenties, that on his return from a Boston visit Ottawa seemed very dull, and that he suffered there from a very real emotional and critical starvation. But his fellow-poets, Carman and Roberts, were not entirely benefited by their sojourn in New York, nor would

Lampman have been. What he needed was the enlightenment but not the life of a metropolis.

Even in his youth he had few illusions regarding poetic Bohemianism. Those were the days of the influence of Byron, Shelley and Whitman. There was a strange absence of repression in the air, new notions of man's place in society, of his relation to God, of Biblical higher criticism, of revolutionizing discoveries in science. Some of his Canadian friends even tended toward the new individualism in manners and dress, so admirably satirized in:

> "Mine eyes are blue,
> Byronic hue,
> I turn my collar down.
> Methinks I wear
> The longest hair
> Of any bard in town."

On the contrary, Lampman believed that the greatest poets were first, men of affairs. Æschylus was a soldier and practical patriot; Dante's mind was trained in the great cares of statecraft; Milton could never have written "Paradise Lost" in such a vein without first having been concerned with the affairs of the Commonwealth; and if Byron had been reared in hardihood or called earlier in the life to the Greek Revolution, he might have given to England poetry of greater purpose and power.

Perhaps Lampman lived life too cautiously and took it too seriously. It is true that he respected most of the conventions. But his respectability is not something super-imposed by society; it is the natural expression of a nature too well balanced to be eccentric, too honest to be anything but sincere. There was about him nothing of the poseur. He once said that affectation argued a deficiency in knowledge of human nature, a lack of humanity and of real goodness of heart. Why affect brutality to simulate openness and candour, or unkemptness for abstraction of thought? "A man must be himself most thoroughly before he can enter with real sympathy into the hearts of others." He decried the popular conceptions of the poet as either an unpractical dreamer of fiery disposition, disordered locks and profound remarks, or else an erratic fool with weak eyes, an effeminate drawl, and a predisposition to tears. He pointed out in reality the poet needed to be of an exceedingly practical nature in order to see through the semblances of life to its inner meaning, and to estimate man's proper relation to the universal and the infinite, thus "making him the wisest, manliest, most self contained and even the austerest and apparently most unimpassionable of all men." Such poise he found in Tennyson, and when that great man died in 1892, Lampman wrote two sonnets, only one of which was published, on the beauty and majesty of his passing. Elsewhere he said of him: "While he has not the exquisite and unapproachable spontaneity in beautiful creation that Keats possessed, not the strange simplicity of touch which in Woodsworth was so powerfully penetrating, yet he has a kingly and triumphant mastery of versification; a march and sweep of numbers, a perfection and variety of phrase and cadence in which, through the study and practice of a long life, he has far exceeded his masters."

The appointment of a new poet laureate led to much discussion in literary circles and, among others, Swinburne was mentioned. Lampman definitely disliked him both as an artist and a teacher. He admitted, he said, "that everything that Swinburne touched seemed turned to enchanting sound through the beautiful management of words, cadences and forms of metre and stanza, that sometimes his strains were as sonorous as utterances of the Old Testament prophets, and his lyrics were full of riotous melody as the sea for which he had a strange affinity. But his vocabularly was not large, and his range of imagery astonishingly narrow when one remembered the monotonous recurrence of certain set images like day and night, light and darkness, sunrise and sundown." The matter of his verse Lampman found generally impalpable, misty and elusive, so that the reader laid down the poem having had no contact with thought but simply rolling in a sort of musical verbal ecstasy. He had no message, or, if he had one, it was of an intangible system of political and social anarchy. His "Songs before Sunrise" were mere vague communistic chants; mad glorifications of liberty, defining nothing; invocations of the return of Hellenic beauty and freedom. This freedom applied to social conditions became in Swinburne license and unfettered passion. Reason, order, the ways of Christ were disregarded. Thus, as a thinker and a writer, he lacked the deep, calm dignity which is the mark of a master. Lampman could forgive what to him was lack of narrative power, the heavy movement of "Tristram of Lyonesse," even the unhealthy way in which, whenever possible, Swinburne gave a "morally hideous colouring to the original tale." He could praise the tenderness and geniality of the poems about children and childhood, and "Atlanta in Calydon" which he thought soberest and sanest of the longer works. But what Lampman could not condone was that Swinburnian recklessness of thought and form, "that mad abandonment to the rush of music and sensuous vision, which showed that he had never meditated genially and sympathetically upon the homely things of life, was incapable of understanding the most sacred instincts of human nature and thus, through lack of vision, had unsettled the world instead of making for its peace and purity."

Lampman cared little less for Swinburne than for William Morris, who he thought had written too much and too ineffectively. "His greatest work is the 'Earthly Paradise' written somewhat in imitation of Chaucer; but, without Chaucer's blithe geniality and practical wisdom." He said he could not read much of it without weariness; it had no genuine hearty sympathy with life, no dramatic force, no humour and no real pathos. Nothing but William Morris' marvelous diligence could have led to the purposeless construction of the more unreadable "Life and Death of Jason" and the most unreadable "Tales of the Volsungs." And why was all this effort misdirected? he asked. "Because Morris, like Swinburne, was also under a blight of morbid unhealthiness, obsessed with the power and prevalence of material passion and the dreariness of death and old age." "William Morris," he concluded, "has nothing to help the cause of order and divine beauty and peace, and his work can, therefore, hardly be of much lasting interest to mankind."

The greatest of the Pre-Raphaelite school was, in Lampman's opinion, Dante Gabriel Rossetti, of whom he wrote: "In several attributes of the poet he was great; and his work was distinctly original. He had a quick and sensitive imagination, a piercing insight into some sombre and wayward shades of feeling and a rich gift of music, and although his ideas and the emotions with which he deals are often subtle and occult, his style is wonderfully plain and direct." He valued Rossetti's strange disposition to translate the world of thought into one of mystic imagery and, *vice versa*, to regard every material thing as the expression of something inward and spiritual. He found this best exemplified in that one most beautiful poem, "The Blessed Damozel," which though purely visionary, embodied in mystic symbolism the love of men and women. This love to Rossetti could never be wholly mortal and ephemeral, but spiritual and eternal, since the perfect union of earth was but the prelude to a beautiful and mystic condition hereafter. Naturally, Lampman did not like the poems typified in "Jenny," which seemed to him bare, realistic and hopeless, unfortunately only too representative of the school. Another poem, realistic also, but of somewhat greater worth to him, was "The Last Confession," the narrative of one who has loved with Italian fervour and revenged desertion by striking a dagger into the heart of his mistress. "The manner of it is intensely quiet and vivid. There are passages of enormous pathos, with a subtle and terrible insight into the darker working of passion. It is put together with consummate talent, but is, of course in its nature, painful and disagreeable." Lampman, like Rossetti, loved to get back into mediæval days from the vastness and complexity of modern life, to the primary feelings which belong to all ages and races. "But as Rossetti's mind was moody and personal, so his range was narrow. He dealt with little of life, and though what he worked upon was strikingly done—for he was serious and sincere—yet he cannot be called a great poet. The masterly ability to enter into every variety of life was not his, nor that cheerful manliness which is the sign and seal of genial mastership in verse."

It is plain that Lampman was not in sympathy with the Pre-Raphaelites. There are various reasons for this. In training and disposition he valued classic balance, and these poets appeared restless and impatient. In spite of a certain inherited Teutonic sadness, he was progressive, optimistic and constructive, and they seemed to him sad, despondent, and even morbid. His mind was of that simple and pure type in which only can spring the true renaissance of wonder. "True art," he said, "must be naive." Pre-Raphaelism seemed to him self-conscious, feverish and unmanly. He believed, too, that through generations of law-making, mankind has fashioned for its experience laws which have become as much a part of human nature as the primal instincts are. These laws the Pre-Raphaelites seemed to forget, and instead to give free indulgence to those instincts which it had been the business of society to soften and command. "They have sung for us the extremes of joy and pain," he said, "but never anything of manful trust or hearty endurance, or if they ever have preached restraint and endurance it has been a hang-dog stoicism wearing the yoke about its neck. All this is very useless to us, and it seems to me that the modern school cannot have much permanent influence upon taste, for the one grand reason that they have done nothing to help mankind in the gradual and eternal movement toward order and divine beauty and peace."

Lampman was always interested in the technical side of the writer's art. He himself used many verse forms and his ear was so carefully tuned to the music of poetry that he became a discriminating judge of it in the work of others. But this flair for technique never influenced him unduly in criticism. His final and chief criterion always came back to "Does this man contribute to the welfare of humanity? Has he contact with life?" For this reason he could never identify himself with the cult of Shelley worshippers who came especially to the fore at the time of the centenary of the poet's birth in 1892. Campbell said that to be a poet was to be freed from the trammels of earth so as to discern beauty better and that, as such, Shelley was "a paler, more ethereal Shakespeare." Lampman felt that he lacked "the human." "The world and its life floated before him," he wrote, "not as the substance of reality but as a glorious and awful vision, full of seductive vistas, peaks strangely lighted, and gulfs of profound and terrible darkness. We miss in him that earthly human heartiness and neighbourly warmth of touch which render Shakespeare so imperishably beloved to all tender hearts of men; the quality that glows in Keats' and Wordsworth's best, and lends the sweetest charm to the greater poets of our age."

Of all contemporary poets Matthew Arnold was Lampman's favorite, and him he read more than any other. This was doubtless due to that classic atmosphere which would have suited Lampman's taste, and to that seriousness of outlook, that view of the writer's mission as an emancipator of society which was so characteristic of the Victorian era. In Arnold he found a rare combination of poetry and philosophy which placed him upon a plane unattained by any other in that generation. "It is not the brilliancy, the versatility, the fecundity or the ingenuity of a poet," he said, "that makes him 'great'; it is the plane on which his imagination moves, the height from which he looks down, the magnitude of his ideas." Thus, though Dryden, because of his "great intellectual power, great literary activity and an admirable range of accompaniment" was once considered greater than Milton, the grandeur and breadth of imagination made Milton superior. So, too, Lampman felt his generation somewhat deluded by the dash, the daring and immense cleverness of Byron, and a little too much dazzled by the supreme literary gift of Tennyson and Browning's insight, vigour and extraordinary versatility. But when he read Matthew Arnold he felt that he had reached the hills, and that the time would come when Arnold would be regarded as "the greatest poet of his generation and one of the three or four noblest that England has produced." Upon this subject Lampman and Campbell by no means agreed, for the latter contended that the business of poetry is not mere thought but inspiration, and that, great as Matthew Arnold and Emerson were as thinkers, they merely "poetised the philosophy of history." "They recognized man as a unit in history," said Campbell, "but they knew nothing of him as a living soul."

Next to Arnold, Lampman probably read Keats most thoroughly, for he was especially interested in him as a stylist, and his own early work is often like Keats' in form and thought. After considering all the famous sonnets in English literature, he came to the decision that the most beautiful one was the last which Keats wrote on shipboard in the English Channel, which begins: "Bright star would I were steadfast as thou art." Over it he exclaims: "How tender, how eloquent, how serene. Surely no young poet ever took leave of this troublesome life—this skein of so sweet and bitter destinies—with a purer or sweeter note upon his lips." Perhaps in this choice he may have been influenced not only by his unusual affinity for Keats but also by some haunting premonition of his own early death.

Lampman was especially impressed with the youthful work of Keats and the enormous strides he made in the three years after the publication of his first book. Those first years, like his own, were full of doubts and self-distrust, but his work and confidence improved under the pressure of that searching and insatiable self-criticism which Lampman believed was the surest indication of greatness in a poet.

Of the two famous statements of Keats, "Beauty is truth, truth beauty" and "A thing of beauty is a joy forever," he said one might go further and say that beauty is goodness as well as truth, for he believed that whatever creation of the human imagination is genuinely beautiful is produced by an impulse derived from and akin to the Divine Creator Himself. His own sonnet, "Beauty," is a further development of his thought.

Naturally, the classical element in Keats was to Lampman the echo of a long-loved strain. Keats knew nothing of Greek and little of Latin, but by the sheer force of his sense of beauty he made antiquity live again. Lampman made an attempt to do the same in his "An Athenian Reverie." Moreover Keats was able in the "Eve of St. Agnes" to achieve in an entirely different genre and period a success which Lampman may also have had in mind when he wrote "The Monk" and "Easter Eve." He traced in "Endymion" some of the influence of Ben Jonson's "Sad Shepherd" and Spenser's "Faerie Queene" and in "Hyperion" suggestions of Milton's sonorous notes.

A quality of Keats which endeared him still more to Lampman was his lack of sympathy with the art that aims only to excite, that deals with the abnormal and the passionate. Both poets believed that there is a sacred and eternal use in poetry. It must be clear, spontaneous and inevitable. It must not startle or amaze. It must be unobtrusive. It must be cheerful. For only this is it in accord with a divine beauty and a universal harmony.

Between his favorites, Keats and Matthew Arnold, Lampman felt that he saw a similarity in a desire to maintain an open and flexible mind, free from dogma, creed or formula. Whether this is true or not, undoubtedly Lampman avoided identifying himself with any school which might lead to limitations or the disproportionate view of life resulting from following a philosophy or doctrine. He was not much concerned with the institutions of the church or fraternal societies, and he generally avoided writing poetry which might be considered didactic or doctrinaire. Yet he had very definite moral standards to which he thought poetry should conform. Further, he praised that objectivity in Keats which so contrasted with the subjectivity of Wordsworth and Shelley, and which made him, in Lampman's opinion, the most Shakespearian genius since Shakespeare

Keats said a poet had no real identity, because if of the right sort he was continually being somebody else. Emerson declared that to hold one view one day and another the next was but a sign of open-mindedness and progress. On this Lampman wrote: "Let none quarrel with the poet for this variableness of mood; in fact it is his chiefest charm; it is that which brings him into the most tender and intimate relation with the general soul of humanity." Once, for instance, on returning home at the end of the day, tired and harassed, by some money matter which had more than ever convinced him of the callousness and brutality of business, he wrote:

THE CUP OF LIFE

One after one the high emotions fade;
Time's wheeling measure empties and refills
Year after year; we seek no more the hills
That lure our youth divine and unafraid,
But swarming on some common highway, made
Beaten and smooth, plod onward with blind feet,
And only where the crowded crossways meet
We halt and question, anxious and dismayed.
Yet can we not escape it; some we know
Have angered and grown mad, some scornfully laughed;
Yet surely to each lip—to mine to thine—
Comes with strange scent and pallid poisonous glow
The cup of Life, that dull Circean draught,
That taints us all, and turns the half to swine.

But with morning came a change of mood. He looked out through the sunshine, flooding his doorstep to the great elm "whose vast level fleece of pendent draperies seemed afloat upon the air," and in a new spirit of happiness composed the poem which begins:

"I love the bare earth and all
That works and dreams thereon."

Such is poetic variability, and such variability is capable of contradistinctions. In Keats it is variability of personality, in Emerson of conviction, in Lampman of mood.

Although Lampman with his excellent background of Greek and Latin and his talent, natural and acquired, for verse might very well have undertaken some work of translation, he did not do so. At the same time he was alive to the value of good translations and familiar with many of the most famous. For instance, he said: "Those who are unable to read originals and even those who are, must be eternally grateful to Dryden for the 'Aeneid,' a noble rendering despite many faults; to old Chapman whose Homer still towers heavily over so many a more ambitious attempt; to Edward Fitzgerald for the 'Rubaiyat'; to Rossetti for his one translation from Villon; and to Swinburne for some others; to Emma Lazarus and James Thompson for several translations from Heine, particularly those of the former, who by a subtle affinity of genius and perhaps of race, seems to have taken upon her tongue to an unusual degree the accent of the original. Dante is said to have been very ably translated by Charles Elliot Norton, and even the old translation by Carey must convey to us something more than the bare tissue of the Italian. We owe Coleridge a good deal for the Wallenstein, Goethe has been translated, but surely not adequately and nearly all the rest of the vast field remains unturned save in the clumsiest and most unsightly manner."

Lampman was too wise ever to attempt to define poetry, to cage within a sentence the winged spirit of verse, but it interested him to consider what others thought. It had been defined as the "Interpretation of the Invisible" and again as the "Criticism of Life." He inclined to believe that it was something more than these two and that it was rather, in the words of Alfred Austin, "The

Transfiguration of Life," that is, life surrounded with the halo of the imagination. In view of this definition, it becomes necessary in estimating a poet's worth to ask, is the light of his imagination true, and is the life which he transfigures real? Now the one feature which Lapman always insisted on as the characteristic of the right view of life was its optimism. He read in the history of the human race this rule: that in spite of its half-human half-bestial nature and its many changes and many failures, the human spirit through eternal yearning toward order, beauty and peace was actually progressing. Any literature which did not in the end express or contribute to this progress he did not believe was great literature or could last long in the regard of mankind. For this reason he thought little of dilettantism, realism for its own sake, and especially morbid introspection. To be great was, among other things, to be happy.

Moreover, he considered that other attributes of a great writer were vivacity, versatility and geniality. All the great poets were versatile. Keats could write in a different vein as the reflective antiquity of the "Ode to a Grecian Urn" and the rich, mediæval elaboration of the "Eve of St. Agnes." Tennyson could transfigure life in such varying conditions as in "The Lady of Shalott", the "Lotos-Eaters" and the "Talking Oak." They could do this because they had no personal limitations of thought or feeling but could sing out of the midst of the inner spirit the many conditions of man's happiness and pain. That is why Lampman, so seldom dictatorial, made bold to prophesy that "Longfellow, with his gentle sweetness and occasional insipidity, will be remembered when Poe for all his strange and fascinating power will be forgotten. Matthew Arnold's 'Forsaken Merman' will live when all the beautiful insanity of Swinburne is spoken of no longer."

It is gratifying to see how catholic, if discriminating, Lampman was in his tastes and how international in his interests, in writing of de Maupassant's then weakening brain; of the bed-ridden Heine with Stoic power still playing upon things "with that Titanic lightning flash of his wit"; of Tolstoi, "the greatest after Shakespeare in his vast and subtle knowledge of the human heart"; of Maeterlinck, just then called the Belgian Shakespeare; of Renan dying poor with "the poet's sovereign indifference to wealth."

The quarrel between realism and romanticism seemed to Lampman about as empty as that over the iota in the Nicene creed. "If a writer's work have the charm of beauty, the convincing power of sincerity, the kindling fire of enthusiasm or if it propels the mind along mightier avenues of thought, opens wider breadths of vision, or plants in the heart the seed of a juster and more tender humanity, what matter whether his method be that of one or the other?" It seemed to him that every writer of real gift was a realist in so far as his characters live and move according to the actual world. He quoted "Rob Roy" and "Old Mortality" and the books of Dickens, Thackeray and Charles Reade as "enchanted worlds, with their delightful people quite as real as one's next door neighbour and probably more companionable." "When I read 'Middlemarch' and 'Daniel Deronda'," he said, "and consider the intellect that planned those two books, the insight, the imaginative grasp and the fervid and compassionate wisdom that possess them and makes them in every sentence a revelation and a stimulus, it seems a miserable impertinence to find fault even with the least detail of form or execution."

Another literary practice with which Lampman had little patience was the scholarly game of source hunting. Apropos of a suggested provenience of a passage trom

Tennyson's "Passing of Arthur," from the fourth book of the Odyssey, Lampman said: "The blind book-worm never realizes that it is possible for two strong imaginations even at a distance of many centuries to happen upon the same image without ever having communicated with one another in the remotest way."

Likewise he had no patience with the practice of authors who pampered to the public sense of curiosity by publishing articles on how they came to write their most popular books. To him the author's high calling was too fine a thing to be paraded before the public gaze. He believed that a man's best work was the fruit of silent and patient concentration in a seclusion far from the public concern and, much as he valued recognition and would have been encouraged doubtless by more, he did make a practise of writing out of the best that was in him and he, and not the public, was the severest critic.

Once he investigated the writing methods of great men of the past. Addison, he found, was supposed to have written as he paced up and down a long room at each end of which was placed a decanter of wine. Many of Wordsworth's poems were composed as he walked a secluded path near his house at Rydal. Tennyson wrote indoors, in his study, with his pipe and an open fire for company. Poe roamed about the house fretting like a caged beast. Keats wrote very easily beneath the trees or lying on a grassy bank. Lampman, especially in earlier days, planned to devote a certain part of each day or rather night to writing. Yet he did not believe that anyone could sit squarely down with a sheet of paper before him and write poetry. He, too, liked to be on the move, and found that the gentle exercise of walking about the room as he smoked, quieted his nerves and helped him to concentrate upon composition. A small note book is in existence in which he jotted down—apparently while on his rambles—certain effects of colour and light but these are so indefinite as to be practically negligible, and it is more probable that he stored within his memory those impressions from the fields to become later the stuff of which verse is made. Very probably, too, much actual composition took place upon his walks. Odd lines were scribbled in note books. In more advanced stages of completion, his poems were written in pencil in school exercise books, and from these they were transferred into permanent form in ink, written in his clear, flowing handwriting.

On the question of inspired writing he took exception to Howells, who had said that nothing ever done in an impulsive mood amounted to anything. Lampman believed that though a certain amount of routine was inevitable, many a book was better for having portions written under the stimulus of excitement, and he pointed out that the reaction which follows such excitement in the writer, sometimes makes him incapable of judging his work with sufficient optimism. He was, from his college days, a very facile versifier but although many of his poems were doubtless readily written as is indicated by the large number produced during certain periods, they were carefully corrected, and even an utterance so apparently spontaneous as "Peccavi, Domine," had single lines changed three or four times before they were satisfactory.

In a summary of Lampman's powers as a literary critic the most striking feature is the combined breadth and sanity of his taste, supported by his very careful and conscientious study of the subject. He was evidently quite unprejudiced by national considerations, and could estimate American, British or native writers without bias —not an easy matter in days when there was a tendency to decry American talent and to praise Canadian writers unduly. It is true that he had certain personal predilections as in favour of Matthew Arnold and against the Pre-Raphaelite School and that in keeping with the moralistic spirit of the times, he was concerned with writers not alone as writers but as emancipators. But his criticism is not much deflected by these considerations; most of it hits the mark fairly and is as true now as when it was written.

Moreover, Lampman as a critic reveals himself differently and in an even clearer light than as a poet. His thoughts are less projected into a region of sublimated art, more personal and intimate. Reading them, and not his poetry, one sees those qualities which occasionally made him so brilliant in literary talk and argument. More than this, his criticism shows him a student familiar with Elizabethan as well as Victorian literature, shows that he could write soundly of American sonnets or the great translations, make distinctions between Thoreau and Emerson or realism and romanticism, quote Aeschylus, Dante, Milton and Byron in confirmation of a point. He was not primarily a critic, but his poetry and personality take on an added interest in view of his opinions of the writings of other men.

CHAPTER XI.

NATURE.

AMPMAN was preëminently the poet of Canadian nature. He knew it intimately, described it accurately, interpreted it with insight and imagination. It inspired his best work and gave him a place unequalled before or since in that field of the literature of his native land.

As a disciple of Beauty, he found in its contemplation not only sensuous pleasure and a mood conducive to thought, but also a guarantee of happiness. Nothing except his fellow creatures, he said, can ever bore a man who has learned the satisfaction of contemplating a tree, a field, a flower, or a blade of grass. Pessimism is impossible. The world of nature is at his feet. True, people do sometimes put up irritating signs which read "No trespassing," but to the scientist, the artist, and the poet this world belongs to no one in particular, and one of these may make more for humanity out of the land than the owner or his descendants may ever do. Beauty is not only in the Rocky Mountains, or the Yosemite Valley; it is in the next field. Not unlike Rousseau's was Lampman's belief that nothing in nature is ugly either in itself or in its relations to its surroundings, and that any other condition is due to the perverting hand of man. Naturally, he scorned the human impulse to go into the woods with rod and gun. Even the botanist he thought only half legitimate in his attitude towards nature. He wanted every man to be a John Burroughs or a Bradford

Torrey, or, still better, a loafer with an open heart and a perceptive eye.

Even stronger than his feeling against needless killing of wild life, was his aversion to the destruction of wild flowers. He lamented the disappearance of the pine forests, the buffalo and the wild pigeon, and he was determined that a like fate should not befall the flowers. Once someone confided to him a place near Ottawa where the golden lady's slippers still grew in profusion. When he went and saw them there, "standing in little companies in the pools in the moist, rocky soil, with shafts of the afternoon sun shining in upon them," he carried only two or three away and kept faithfully the secret of their haunt.

He had a horror of stuffed birds, and when the management of the World's Fair in Chicago offered a prize in taxidermy, he protested that it would lead to much needless destruction.

The song birds were his never ending study and delight, and some of his most striking lines describe bird songs, for instance, in "April Voices," "The blackbirds . . . wheezing and squeaking in discordant glee." Elsewhere the crow "banters and chides," the robin "flutes," the hermit thrush "pours his golden music," the high-ho "shouts," and the bobolink "sprinkles his music about the meadows." Again there sounds in his poetry "the shore-lark's brittle song," the "silver-piping sparrow," the "rich-throated thrush," "the jibing cry" of the jay, and the "querulous outcry of the loon." One of his first appearances in print was in "Bird Voices," published in the "Century Magazine," May, 1885:

"The robin and the sparrow a-wing in silver-throated accord;
The low soft breath of a flute, and the deep short pick of a chord.
A golden chord and a flute, where the throat of the oriole swells
Fieldward, and out of the blue the passing of bobolink bells."

Better still is that other striking figure in "At Dusk":

> "And now the whip-poor-will,
> Beyond the river margins, glassed and thinned,
> Whips the cool hollows with his liquid note."

He regretted never having heard the English nightingale or skylark, but thought that "not even in England have they as great a variety of dainty and appealing voices as are to be met with on any summer day in Canadian fields—the song-sparrow, the robin and the blue-bird that come before the wild-flower and the trilium, the vesper-sparrow, tenderest and most lyric of singers, whose song seems most touching and most in season as his name implies, when we hear it from the dusky, scarce distinguishable fields at evening; the bobolink, who is the merry, love-making, gay-coated cavalier of our breezy meadows, forever joyous and alert, thinking that his life is intended for nothing but the old-fashioned troubadour business of singing rondeaus and villanelles to one's lady love; the white-throated sparrow, the piper of that strange, clear, long-drawn, meditative note that comes to us from the swamp or clearing and embodies the very mood of him who whiles away a long May day in idle stroll and meditation; the grave thrushes; the veery with his revolving metallic note having something in it like the sound of shot running round and round in a gun barrel, a note suggestive of mid-summer and quiet heat; the hermit, according to Burroughs, the finest of our songsters, whose distant, lingering music, heard in the forest depths or from the untilled mountain-side is the very voice of the spirit of solitude, laden with the memories of forgotten flowers, and fading away into silence and shadow as remote and spectral as they are; the wood-thrush, not so common with us, and the brown thrush, a singer of great energy and variety; the cat-bird, the vivacious mimic and eccentric songster; the pee-weet with its peculiar infantine, appealing note; the great high holder or high-ho, whose jolly, flute-like laughter rings far away out of the woodside or the rough field; the drawling pipe and silvern splutter of the meadow-lark; and many another of the warblers, fly-catchers, vireos, and the rest too numerous to recount." His own preference was for the vesper sparrow. He listened "at morning and evening for its abandon, its tenderness, its lyrical gush" and if he did not hear it, missed something that tempered his thoughts "with a gentle and humane emotion."

Lampman, like many present-day Canadians regretted that the marvellous and irreplaceable timber lands had been so ruthlessly cut over in the early days before governmental steps were taken towards fire prevention and the conservation of national parks. He expressed himself in strong terms against the government's apathy toward tree preservation in his day. "An ancient and close-grown pine forest," he said, "is a wonderful spectacle, and its effect upon the imagination is something not produced by any other thing in the world. I never see a sawlog afloat on one of our rivers without a pang, not because I would not have logs cut, but because I know that the trees must all go; must all perish irrevocably." Indeed the trees took on a sort of personality, even nationality for him. The oak was British, the elm Italian in grace, the pine the most eery, inspiring, and Celtic of the lot. It was the priest of the forest, leading his thoughts up and out into "regions of exquisite purity and repose." He would trudge a whole half day along the road to reach a pine woods, for there as if by magic he soon ceased to be troubled by petty cares and "Time and all the pine-groves of the world" seemed to enfold his spirit in their power. He was soothed by their pungent smell and by the wind droning or roaring through their branches, and his imagination was especially quickened by the sight of a single sentinel standing dark against a sunset or by the gloomy, mysterious masses of distant pine groves in a twilight landscape. This same Anglo-Saxon melancholy attaches itself to cedars as well, who "moan in dusky-skirted lines strange answers of an ancient runic call." And in the earliest Spring:

> "A few bronzed cedars in their fading dress
> Almost asleep for happy weariness,
> Lean their blue shadows on the puckered snow."

Though Lampman's poetry by actual count contains more references to pines than to any other trees, he also describes the maples, elms, poplars, beeches and fruit trees. He appealed to people to plant the latter not only for use but beauty as well, because, though the wild scenery of the forest is beautiful, there is an equal if different loveliness about an orchard, implying as it does, the care of preceding generations. Some of the best scenes in his "Story of an Affinity" take place in an orchard in which there is a special tree called Margaret's. He had spent many happy days, as a boy with his uncle in Thorold in the Niagara peninsula, which has long been noted as the finest orchard district of Ontario. Sometimes in his poetry there are glimpses of pink and white cherry blossoms, or plum trees misty and blue-grey, and once, in May, he comes upon a leaf-paven pool beyond which stands "a plum tree in full blow, creamy in bloom and humming like a hive."

Of course, no Canadian, poet or otherwise, can be unaffected by that feature of Canadian landscape which is so unique, the colouring of the trees in Autumn. Sometimes they are "broken beeches tangled with wild vine," sometimes yellowing elm trees, sometimes flaming maples. In "Autumn Maples" the various colours are quaintly attributed to different emotions. Some are "beaconing clouds of flame" afire upon the hills, some yearing upon the sunset have blushed for very shame, while:

> "Others for very wrath have turned a rusty red
> And some that knew not either grief or dread,
> Ere the old year should find its iron close,
> Have gathered down the sun's last smiles acold,
> Deep, deep, into their luminous hearts of gold."

In the "Lake in the Forest," so reminiscent of Temagami, there is a less original but more imaginative figure of the trees as:

> "Thy maskers that make revel for an hour,
> In gold and ruby, till the blighting power
> Strips them, and all their rustling braveries
> In urns and earthen caskets lays away."

Lampman was always fond of investing the trees with personality and emotion, as did the more fantastic Emily Dickinson. For instance:

> "Not far to fieldward in the central heat,
> Shadowing the clover, a pale poplar stands
> With glimmering leaves that, when the wind comes, beat
> Together like unnumerable small hands."

Again, the poplars are "silver tasseled," or "gold green, laughing in their hearts." The elms are almost always "swaying" or "pendulent" or "thatched and plumed with green." In advancing Spring the maples are "full of little crimson knots," the twigs and branches of the birch are "shooting into little emerald flames" and quaintest of all,

> "The maple leaves are spreading slowly out
> Like small red hats or pointed parasols."

It was Miss Matty's farmer lover in "Cranford" who asked its author the colour of ash buds in March. He had lived in the country all his life, he told her, and had never known the answer until the poetry of a young man (Tennyson) told him they were black. Lampman's treatment of trees is remarkable for two things: for the play of his imagination making them now tortured souls, now happy children; and for the flashes of genius in which, in a word, he gives the very picture, born of accurate observation.

Yet Lampman was not only a poet and a naturalist but a pictorial artist as well. Although he tried outdoor sketching only a little, many of his poems were like pictures; he had various artist friends, and he was much interested in the pictures and the progress of art in the Dominion.

During his time the National Gallery of Canada, at Ottawa, was forming under government supervision, a collection of pictures by European and American artists which should give inspiration by example and encouragement by purchase to native artists. To just what extent these purchases should be foreign was always a debatable point. Although anxious that Canadians should sell their pictures, Lampman advocated a government appropriation of fifty thousand dollars annually for the purchase of foreign works of art, because he felt that education in art, as in literature and music, was a matter not so much of instruction as of inspiration, and that there was more education in a great inspiring model than in a hundred schools. Moreover, he was wise to see that in painting as in the other arts, Canadians could not afford to be provincial but must be open to influence which was world wide. At the same time he followed with great interest the work of the Canadians. Charles Moss, the Ottawa painter, was a personal friend and a frequent visitor at his house and companion of his walks. He was early in his appreciation of Homer Watsons' landscapes. Some times he wrote reviews of the annual Academy Exhibitions in Ottawa. In that of 1892 he mentioned Homer Watson's shadowy fields, Franklin Brownell's "Low Tide," and George Reid's "Foreclosure of the Mortgage," a narrative picture which was favourably received at the Chicago World's Fair. Given his choice, he would have chosen pictures by Watson, Brownell, Brymner, O'Brien, Woodcock, Fowler, Manly and Mrs. Reid.

The great crux in any national art is to make it typically local and at the same time universal in its outlook and appeal. In his poetry Lampman strove for this, and felt that Canadian painters had a great and comparatively unbroken field before them, especially in the interpretation of winter landscape. Just by way of proving it, he sketched in, with skilful pen-strokes the following picture in prose: "In the winter dawn, with every gradation of red and gold and blue; even in the early forenoon, when the towers of our northern capital stand westward pale and luminous, touched with rose, against a pale greenish-blue sky, when every roof fronting the sun is a sheet of dazzling cream and every roof not sunlit and every shadow a patch of the clearest crystaline violet; in the coming of winter night with its gorgeous changes of colour, subtle and indescribable, what an infinite variety of choice there is for the hand of the painter, yet how simple in many cases, yet always how perfect the beauty with which he would have to deal." Such sentences set one wondering whether in Lampman the poet was not lost a potential painter, but after all, these pictures in his verse, flashing with colour and light, are quite as lasting, almost as vivid and less static in words than in paint. What is the following but a detailed study, which might be called "Autumn Stream": "It is at this season that the streams, those streams that loiter slowly through the low-lying meadows—put on their utmost beauty.

Bordered by trees and exposed in little reaches to the sun, the golden heats and full shadows of Autumn lie upon them. The bitter-sweet hangs from the close branches of the alder and ripens its berries. Innumerable water weeds and mosses float and sway in the sluggish stream, and the swift spiders upon its surface flit hither and thither, throwing their spotted shadows upon the bottom. The loose-strife, knotted with ruby bloom, curves down its willowy stems to meet the water. Masses of blooming plants line its edges: golden rod in slender groves arching into gold; purple bone-set or trumpet weed in whose soft, woolly heads the bees love to trample and burrow; tall stems of chelone or turtle-head with their white spout-like blossoms; tangled drifts of white-starred bed-straw; jewel weed in delicate profusion of translucent stems and rich-tinted sensitive bloom; cloudy spots of white snake-root; tufts of closed gentian whose long corollas that never open the bumble bees spread asunder with their feet, thrust themselves into and almost disappear. These with patches of yarrow, many shades and sizes of aster, delicate blossoms of arrowhead that seem made of snowflakes that melt as you look at them, and an occasional bed of purple pickerel-weed springing from the shallow edge of the water, almost cover and conceal the little stream in their wild vigour of growth and mingled splendour of colour. It is in the midst of some such scene as this, in the late August afternoon, when the sun sets hot upon the harvest fields, and the woods are deep with mellow glooms, and the elms cast long shadows, that the season seems to present herself to us like a divine personality in all the gracious joy of her prime and the calm consciousness of a perfect achievement."

Of course, it is to Lampman's poetry that one looks for the most perfect expression of himself as a pictorial artist. Here the colour, light and atmospheric effects are exceedingly authentic and often startlingly beautiful. He has a fondness for pastel colours in which gold, green, silver and gray predominate, with usually a dash of rose. In "April" for instance,

> "The creamy sun at even scatters down
> A gold-green mist across the murmuring town."

His distances are especially beautiful. Sometimes at the far-off violet hills are "horizons filmed with showers"; sometimes the clouds are "fleeces dull as horn"; again, across the blue are drawn "thin pale threads like streaks of ash"; while typical of an Ottawa landscape is:

> "The vast gray church that seems to breathe
> In heaven with its dreaming spire."

Day-break naturally takes on more brilliant colour, as in the sonnet "Sirius":

> "The old night waned and all the purple dawn
> Grew pale with green and opal."

Then later as morning advances:

> "The sun down the long mountain valley rolled
> A sudden swinging avalanche of gold."

Sunset is the most brilliant time of all. In "The City" the sun, grown darker than gold, sets in clouds of crimson, rose and amethyst. Again, a purple red line above the pine-fringed horizon softly melts into an olive sky. "Winter Hues Recalled" contains one of his most gorgeous sunsets: "The whole broad west was like a molten sea of crimson," in the north the hills were veiled in "a mist of rose," while from the sapphire shadows of the valley rose the sun-gilded towers of the city like clusters of mauve amethysts.

Nor is Lampman entirely a colourist. The following

sonnet shows not only his colour sense but fine discrimination in light gradations:

A SUNSET AT LES EBOULEMENTS.

Broad shadows fall. On all the mountain side
The scythe-swept fields are silent. Slowly home
By the long beach the high-piled hay-carts come,
Splashing the pale salt shallows. Over wide
Fawn-coloured wastes of mud the slipping tide,
Round the dun rocks and wattled fisheries,
Creeps murmuring in. And now by twos and threes,
O'er the slow spreading pools with clamorous chide,
Belated crows from strip to strip take flight.
Soon will the first star shine; yet e'er the night
Reach onward to the pale-green distances,
The sun's last shaft beyond the gray sea-floor
Still dreams upon the Kamouraska shore,
And the long line of golden villages.

The night is full of fascination though not of colour. In "Uplifting," the night sky is "sable and glittering like a mystic shield." Nor does the moon simply rise—it "shines like burnished gold," "above the world's dark border burns yellow and large," is " a slender queen", or, again "a curved olive leaf of gold." "Sirius" is a sonnet of moon and stars and earliest daybreak, described with beauty and power:

"The silvered bow
Of broad Orion still pursued the night
And farther down amid the gathering light
A great star leaped and smouldered."

From skies and distances, Lampman turns to the earth with its fields, forests and rivers, the plants, animals and men. In fields and forests he excels in broad colour effects; plants and individual trees are described with a few deft colour strokes; birds and animals are often presented in a fantastic fashion; the few people introduced into the picture are either to add a colour note as were the figures of Corot, or in other cases for life and humour.

Lampman's fields are "golden meadows," "emerald seas of verdure fading on to far-off shores of turquoise," or plains buried in the "blind white glare" of snow.

The colour which occurs more frequently than any other throughout his nature verse is gold, and it is evident that he is fond of metallic colours, silver, gray, steely blue, and less frequently, brown, black and amber. "Winter Evening" is a study in gold—the houses, chimneys, plains, stars, even the breath from the nostrils of the horses, are of that glittering colour. In marked contrast, "Autumn Waste" is a poem in monochrome. Here a grey sky broods over cold grey waters, bare paths, and melancholy lands. Similarly, in "April Night":

> "The river with its stately sweep and wheel
> Moves on slow-motioned, luminous, gray like steel."

Elsewhere Lampman's rivers run "pale silver," "burnished," "dark brown," "dull blue" when covered with ice, and even black. In stilless they are "like a mirror, purple gray"; in logging time, "amber, streaked with foam"; once "bluer than the sky," but for the most part rarely bright or dancing.

His poetry is rich in plants and flowers, and he uses the same exquisite care in describing them, coupled with a growing feeling for the fantastic as he leaves the grander aspects of sky and field. In dealing with plants he had a noticeable fondness for fire. The buttercups are sparks gliding through the grass, the loose-strife burns like a ruby, the blood-root kindles at dawn her spiral taper of snow, while the vervain is like a many-branched candlestick lit with violet flame. There are examples, too, of a pretty fancy in clothing the plants like people:

> "Last year's sedges scold
> In some drear language, rustling haggardly
> Their thin dead leaves and dusky hoods of gold."

Behold also:

> "The creamy blood-root in her suit of gray."

In brighter colours are the purple-fringed heads of the bee-sought flowers, the full-ribbed orange pumpkin, and in Spring the thin, green spears of wheat. The golden-rod is a green forest "yellowing upward into gold" and is beautiful even in death with its pale gray shadowy plumes of Autumn.

Most pictures take on added interest when they contain not only colour but life. In Lampman's there are belted bees; a locust like a jester capering in his cloak of gray; a dragon fly, "azure glint and crystal gleam," and sleek red horses in September sunlight. His people include "tawny river dogs" poling the rafts down the river; hay-makers, "brown of neck and booted gray"; an old woman gathering strawberries; a group of plodding snowshoers; the stooped figure of a ploughman for all the world like a Millet peasant, and the jovial wintry lumbermen:

> "With their cheeks as red as flannel,
> And their beards as white as foam."

There are unreal people in Lampman's poetry as well. June sits by a stream waist-deep in white ænemones. Sweet Summer falls asleep. Autumn a wizard, faint, blue-eyed goes swinging his censer through the land. Earth, an old man sits dreaming unconscious of the wild outrider the Wind, which will soon be upon him heralding the approach of Winter and his Frost Spirits who come to mock at men.

There are, too, glimpses of ancient classic deities as well:

> "At morning we shall catch the glow
> Of Dian's quiver on the hill,
> And somewhere in the glades I know
> That Pan is at his piping still."

And for a moment in "June" one sees:

> "Psyche, the white-limbed goddess, still pursued,
> Fleet footed as of yore,
> The noonday ringing with her frighted peals,
> Down the bright sward and through the reeds she ran,
> Urged by the mountain echoes, at her heels
> The hot-blown cheeks and trampling feet of Pan."

To regard Lampman merely as a poetic picture maker, a recorder of sound and colour, of plant and animal life, a peopler of the woods with Titans or dryads would be to omit the most important feature of his Nature, its philosophical aspect. For, careful as he was to avoid didacticism in his poetry, there is still a very definite thought, a delicate philosophy of life.

To him Nature, though sometimes an enigma, was more often a consolation, an inspiration, and a teacher.

The figure of Earth as mother occurs frequently in his poetry. In "The Frogs" she chooses them to pipe for her that men may know her mood; in "Freedom" her children commune with her, bound closely by the thrall of her beauty; in "A Prayer" she is besought for some little of her light and majesty; and in "Comfort of the Fields" with

> ". . . cool fair fingers radiantly divine,
> The mighty mother brings us in her hand,
> For all tired eyes and foreheads pinched and wan
> Her restful cup, her beaker of bright wine."

In times of ill-health, discouragement and depression, Lampman looked to Nature for consolation and calm. "Absorb me and fold me round," he exclaimed, "for broken and tired am I." Night brought its healing balm. In the fields in "April," he says he

> "Wandered with happy feet, and quite forgot
> The shallow toil, the strife against the grain,
> Near souls, that hear us call, but answer not,
> The loneliness, perplexity and pain,
> And high thoughts cankered with an earthly stain."

In "April in the Hills" he breaks into a jubilant song of gladness for the recurring Spring. He goes striding through the valleys with new mirth and might in "After Rain." In "Cloud-Break" there is a moment of vision and rejuvenation, and in "The Lake in the Forest," addressing Manitou, the Great Spirit of the Indians, he says:

> "O Maker of the light and sinewy frame,
> The hunters' iron hands and tireless feet;
> O Breath, whose kindling ether, keen and sweet,
> Thickens the thews and fills the blood with flame;
> O Manitou, before the mists are drawn,
> The dewy webs unspun,
> While yet the smiling pines are soft with dawn,
> My forehead greets the sun;
> With lifted heart and hands I take my place,
> And feel thy living presence face to face."

For Lampman, Nature was also a teacher, not in a forced, moralizing fashion but in a very natural way, because to him Nature and Man were one. "We know with the fullest intensity of sympathy," he wrote, "that we are of one birth with everything about us, brethren to the trees, and kin to the very grass that now, even at noon in the shadowy places, flings the dew about our feet." For this reason, somewhat like Shelley in his "Ode to the West Wind," he could address the wind in "Storm" thus:

> "I most that love you, Wind, when you are fierce and free
> In these dull fetters cannot long remain;

Lo, I will rise and break my thongs and flee
Forth to your drift and beating, till my brain
Even for an hour grow wild in your divine embraces,
And then creep back into mine earthly traces
And bind me with my chain."

In "Ode to the Hills" he could wish to derive from them something of their beauty and strength and passionless imperturbability. The humble yarrow could teach him the beauty of the unnoticed, the lilies that simplicity of which Solomon wrote, the warbling vireo the happiness of an uneventful existence. He did not pretend to think that Nature could solve the riddle of life. The flowers in "Sweetness of Life" are born, linger, and die without question. "Thou hast no human soul, O flower" he wrote. But it meant much to him that though "custom and commonwealths and faiths shall pass" the little speedwell would bloom unchanged, that though the maples and elms and birches in "Sapphics" were hastening, like himself, to the autumn of life, in time they would all lie eventually in the same earth, and that

"What is lovely, what sublime,
Becomes, in an increasing span,
One with earth and one with man,
One, despite these mortal scars,
With the planets and the stars."

Perhaps the poem which best sums up Lampman's attitude to Nature, with its soothing, enspiriting, instructing and ennobling influences, is the following sonnet:

ON THE COMPANIONSHIP WITH NATURE.

Let us be much with Nature; not as they
That labour without seeing, that employ
Her unloved forces, blindly without joy;
Nor those whose hands and crude delights obey
The old brute passion to hunt down and slay;

But rather as children of one common birth,
Discerning in each natural fruit of earth
Kinship and bond with this diviner clay.
Let us be with her wholly at all hours,
With the fond lover's zest, who is content
If his ear hears, and his eye but sees;
So shall we grow like her in mould and bent,
Our bodies stately as her blessèd trees,
Our thoughts as sweet and sumptuous as her flowers.

CHAPTER XII.

"LYRICS OF EARTH."

THE summer of 1892, the year following his Boston visit, Lampman and his family spent at a farm house near enough to Ottawa to make commuting possible. There the poet wrote a little and reflected and rested a good deal, bettering his physical condition as much as possible, and there he spent his three weeks' holidays quietly among the hills and meadows, of which he wrote:

> "I watched the gray hawk wheel and drop,
> Sole shadow on the shining world;
> I saw the mountains clothed and curled,
> With forest ruffling to the top;
> I saw the river's length unfurled,
> Pale silver down the fruited plain,
> Grown great and stately with the rain."

When he returned to Ottawa in the Autumn it was to 369 Daly Avenue, one of a row of stone houses much larger than the first home which he had found small to the point of oppression. The new house was a tax both upon his salary and upon the housekeeping energies of his wife, but it gave him what he had not had before, a room in which he could work by himself, undisturbed. Here he completed his second volume of poems and wrote a first dedication to his mother, whose devotion was not unlike that of Ralph Waldo Emerson's mother for her children. He considered for the book the titles of "A Gift from the Sun" and "Pictures and Meditations" before choosing "Lyrics of Earth," the one under which it finally appeared. Houghton, Mifflin and Co. were the first publishers to whom he submitted it, and after keeping him in suspense for four months they returned the manuscript. He then tried Scribner's, who also rejected it. He had a period of ill-luck too, in not selling to the magazines, though "The Youth's Companion" bought "By an Autumn Stream." At this time he received an invitation from Kingston, to deliver a lecture on Keats and his Boston friends, hearing of it, proposed that he repeat it there. At first he considered the venture, but writing of the lecture was delayed by the composition of a long narrative poem which had taken his fancy, and moreover, he hesitated to appear as a lecturer in the United States without being sure that he was in a position to give his best. Lacking the ability to deliver a lecture either extempore or from memory, he doubted its effect if read. That winter he completed the Keats paper, but it was never given in Boston, and though Mr. Scudder, of the "Atlantic Monthly," gave it praise as a lecture he did not buy it. Another proposal was for him to go to Boston as a reader on the staff of "The Youth's Companion," at $1,000 a year. This would have been augmented by his writing, from which he was making at the time at least $300 a year. Had he been alone he would have accepted at once, but he hesitated to subject his wife and child to poverty. He was not unambitious, but his nature was so sensitive and he was so incapable of pushing his interests with men of affairs, that he could not bring himself to make the change, even though the proposed increase in the hours of the Post Office department threatened his precious leisure. Moreover, he felt that the somewhat light drudgery of the government position was performed while his literary faculties were, for the time being, in abeyance, whereas the work of a reader in a magazine office, though requiring the exercise of a writer's powers, would do so in such trivial and uninteresting fashion as to do him in the end, far more injury than if he remained in Ottawa.

Nevertheless he made plans to visit Boston in March, plans which had to be twice altered, first on account of his daughter Natalie's illness and again when for the third successive winter, he fell ill with *la grippe;* a disease which he believed would eventually be fatal to him. Consequently, it was not until April 20th that he visited Boston a second time. After a pleasant visit with his friends, he returned to Ottawa, improved in health and spirits, but with no further prospects of removal. The readership he had declined and the Cornell professorship had long been given up as an improbability. To be sure, Professor Tyler wrote suggesting a position in the Cornell Library, but it did not promise much. Lampman was, in fact, becoming more and more definitely identified with his surroundings, and he was not unhappy in his position save for a feeling that there was something cowardly about continuing in it if it were in his power to be anything better.

That summer he and his family spent in the country. He continued to make efforts to market his book, trying a third publisher in Roberts Brothers, who also returned it. The Mermaid Inn engagement was terminated, making his prospects a trifle poorer. Yet, in spite of this, he continued to read and compose. For the first time, he began reading Balzac and felt his heart going out in sympathy to the characters in a way which never happened when he read the current analytical novelists. His own writing was maintained by the encouragement of a few friends and by the sheer joy of the craft. To have written a good stanza was to experience a thrill, he said, equalled only when a young man's apparently unattainable sweetheart for the first time turns answering eyes upon him. For most criticism he cared little, because it was usually second-hand and like stale wine, had lost all potency, but praise from the discriminating was heartening and a little intoxicating. That summer was an unusually good one for work. Seldom had he been in the verse-making humour so thoroughly and for so long a time. He could divine no cause for it, he said, unless he were going mad, but he believed that if he had the summer free he could have produced some long work of merit. As it was, he wrote a number of short pieces and planned another volume, although the second was still without a publisher, for he now was passing into a new phase, a phase of concern less with nature and more with narrative and human nature. This poetry was perhaps more personal than any he had previously written, although he maintained that he seldom wrote anything as a direct expression of personal feeling uttered in a lyrical way. With this third volume he hoped to be more successful. His friends, Carman and Roberts, were bringing out books, Duncan Campbell Scott had published his "Magic House" and William Wilfred Campbell "The Dread Voyage." Lampman believed that Scott could write better verse than he in some respects, and that the infinite devotion and ambition and, alas, conceit of Campbell would make him bound to succeed.

Only two events served to break the monotony of the summer of 1893; he was promoted to a second class clerkship with a somewhat increased salary, and with his wife and daughter he visited St. Catharines in the Niagara district. As a young man he had spent some time on his uncle's fruit farm there, and the rich beauty of the country inspired the sonnet which he called "A Niagara Landscape."

By this time Natalie was a year and a half old; a beautiful child with silky golden hair, great grey brown eyes and ruddy cheeks, and her struggles with him and her mother and with the English language were a constant source of amusement to her father. He pretended to think her very wilful with her parents and with children older than she, and he used to say that he could not understand how so forceful a young person could have such a meek man for a father. But he perceived a saving quality in her sense of humour, which he hoped would make up for a lack of steadfastness and consistency in himself as a trainer of children.

The active fervour of verse writing in the summer of 1893 gave place in the autumn and winter to a period of despondency such as he had never experienced before. This was due to several causes. In December he suffered his annual attack of *la grippe*, which left him thin and weak. Then his later verse had not received favourable comment. He had written it under what to him seemed a genuine impulse, but his friends thought that poems like "The Settler's Tale," "Intervias," "My Master's Daughter," and "Margaret" were not worthy of him. It seemed to him that he had lost all power of self-criticism, for if his emotion when writing this verse were wrong, then he had no longer any way of judging the merits of his work. He longed to have some authoritative estimate of himself for encouragement or guidance. He knew that some people considered him an unpractical dreamer. He knew that he lived too solitary a life, and yet he could not change it. He was becoming hypochondriacal. The only safe course seemed a return to writing nature poetry. In that at least, he had been successful and yet he had wished to go farther afield into man's region of strife and development, into the unfolding of tale and human character. In that, other poets had been successful, and his own reading and thought prompted him to believe that, there he, too, might have something to say. In spite of this uncertainty, he sent off his third book to Houghton, Mifflin and Co. and worked away painstakingly at his "Story of an Affinity," which he meant to be a test of whether or not he should write narrative verse. It was not that he was stagnating. On the contrary, he was becoming more and more nervous and excitable. His old mood of calm serenity and detachment was giving way to periods of dejection and discouragement, and he was troubled with insomnia. In such moment he wrote one of his most personal poems, "Peccavi Domine":

> "I have had glimpses of thy way,
> And moved with winds and walked with stars,
> But, weary, I have fallen astray,
> And wounded, who shall count my scars?"

He felt that he was passing through a spiritual revolution in which he sometimes suffered agonies, and yet he was thankful that he was able to suffer rather than become insensible and inarticulate. After waiting three months for word from his publishers, he could even say humourously that either they were very slow people or else they were uncommonly fond of his poetry.

In the Spring of 1894 he began to turn his thoughts back to earlier days and to revise some of his first poems. In these the influence of Keats was very apparent. It had taken him, he said, ten years to get quite clear of the spell of that fascinating person, and there were times when he could almost imagine a faint reincarnation of Keats in himself. He began, too, to review his Greek and to plod through some of the plays of Euripides. He thought it worth two or three years of one's life to know even a little Greek. It gave the reader of modern literature an inimitable breadth of thought and beauty, and to the creative artist it was an anchorage from the fads and crazes of the time.

In August of this year a fresh blow fell upon the Lampmans in the death of their four months' old son, Arnold. Never before had the poet had to do with death. He had become particularly attached to the child, and the loss made him fearful lest he lose others near and dear to him. For the first time he experienced a thorough disgust of life, and the poems "White Pansies," "We too shall sleep," "To Death," and "The Vain Fight," arose from the bitterness of that hour.

Earlier in the year Bliss Carman had written to say that in the capacity of literary adviser to Stone and Kimball he would be glad to receive a collection of Lampman poems, with a view to publication. There were long delays during which the American firm did not even answer Lampman's letters, but finally they agreed to publication, if a Canadian house could be induced to buy the plates and bring out a Canadian edition. This, Lampman was unable to bring about, and the project had to be dropped after a year's delay. In the meantime he had conceived the notion that a collection of a hundred poems, called "A Century of Sonnets," might sell, and with heroic persistence sent them to Houghton, Mifflin and Co., who had already rejected two books. When they had returned them, he tried Scribners. It seemed to him that in the end he would never get a publisher. In an isolated place five hundred miles away no one would take notice of him, whereas those who were living and marketing their work near the centres of publication seemed to have no difficulty. He felt forcibly held down and smothered. He did not want fame and notoriety so much as encouragement, and he was tired of being judged by a single book published, years before, in 1888.

Lampman's health during the winter of 1894-5 was the best it had been for some time. In the fall he had made a practice of taking regular exercise—after office hours—a run in the open, returning for a cold bath. In the winter he did some skating and snow-shoeing. He could not do fancy figures upon the ice, but could continue straight ahead almost indefinitely, and one day, with his brother-in-law, skated for ten miles on the Rideau river. He had, as usual, his winter attack of *la grippe*, but it left him with enough sense of humour at least, to refer to himself after the bacteria had finished with him, as a worm-eaten cheese or dried up cod-fish. His wife's health, on the contrary, was very poor. Fortunately they had moved into a larger but more conveniently arranged house in the same row which, though it threatened to ruin him in coal bills, was better for housekeeping.

William Wilfred Campbell by this time had written his two dramas, "Modred" on an Arthurian theme and "Hildebrand," which had, as Lampman said, enough fire and fury to blow up a theatre. Campbell's extraordinary views as to their excellence and the jealousy which was aroused by anything which might seem to minimize his reputation, made him fancy that Lampman had combined with Carman and Roberts to injure him. In reality, though Lampman found him brusque personally, he appreciated the dramatic power of his work. On two occasions Campbell made very broad hints to him of machinations, the injustice of which Lampman naturally resented and he defended himself with some heat. No man would be less likely to plot against Campbell's success than Lampman.

His own luck seemed to be improving in the Spring of '95, when, through E. W. Thomson, the firm of Copeland and Day became interested in his work. He was grateful for his friend's interest and accepted his suggestions for the contents of the book, to put "The Sweetness of Life" first and to make certain omissions, although he wished to retain "Vivia Perpetua," "Ingvi and Alf" and "Chione," which he said he had written out of a natural impulse and with satisfaction to himself. They were, he knew, not the sort of thing expected of him. They were not as good as he had written ten years before, but he sometimes thought that even that early work had been over-estimated. He knew that he was not and had never been as some of his friends had said, a great poet. Greatness, he felt, must spring from qualities which he did not have; from force, fearlessness, brightness. He called himself, in this pessimistic mood, merely a minor poet of a superior order; a man who did not possess his own soul. One Saturday in June, 1895, he was too depressed to go to the office, but made his way instead into the country where, after suffering all that day and most of the next, it gradually came to him, under the sun and sky, that it was really June and that perhaps he was still alive. Even a four weeks' vacation spent in hill-climbing and canoe-paddling did not help much, and the forthcoming book failed greatly to arouse his interest. It meant little to him that he could write decently years ago, he said. What distressed him was his uncertainty as to the quality of his present writing. He hoped that in four years he might manage to retire at the head of his class on a pension of $600 or $700, when in some quiet country place he might give himself over to freedom and poetry. Where he was he felt bound and suffocated, and knew that even with the genius of a Milton he could have done nothing. "It is the slow, not difficult but endless grind of work," he wrote,[1] "that one regards with dull disgust, that really saps one's vitality and takes the spirit out of a man. He may work like a Titan at something which his whole

[1] Letter to Dr. Tait McKenzie from Ottawa, June 28, 1895.

soul inspires, but he ought to be refreshed by his labour which is then no labour but only strenuous play."

In the summer of 1895 he gave up writing altogether and continued his reading of Greek plays, but after an encouraging visit from E. W. Thompson in the autumn, he began a prose essay on "Happiness." He said that he knew it would not sell, for it was a stupid production, but his only hope was that it differed a little from the stupidity in common circulation. He sent it to Scribner's and they returned it. Then, much to his surprise, it was purchased by "Harper's Magazine."

In this essay he began by picturing the three roads open to a man emerging from the period of childhood; that of Pallas Athene, who will preside over the fruitful development of his talents; that of Circe, who allows him full play of the emotions; and a third, unsponsored, which is most frequently followed and which leads to a life of aimless, commonplace routine. Between the happiness of the extreme egoist absorbed in his own powers, and the happiness of the extreme altruist devoted to the cause of others, lies the rare but greatest happiness of the man whose nature is a perfect balance of selfishness and devotion, who lives "at ease, joyous, and untroubled, receiving and conferring pleasure, universally loving and beloved." Such happiness can be attained only by those whose energy finds expression either in the one occupation to which they are most fitted, or, lacking that, in additional creative work. Against the limiting circumstances which hinder self-expression the extremist will rebel, but the wise and truly happy man sees in them, like the poet working within the narrow bounds of the sonnet, a challenge to his skill. A second aid to happiness is a sense of humour which not only makes attractive the eccentricities of others, but prevents a man taking himself too seriously. Finally, though happiness is usually associated with youth, Lampman argued that it is really greatest in middle age, for then the soul is stored with memories to sweeten bitter days. Thus memory and humour, and a sense of a life lived fully, in spite of limitations, for self and others were Lampmans' chief requisites for happiness.

On the other hand, in less optimistic moods he said that he believed he would be happy only when he would cease to care whether he was noticed, loved, or read. The ideal of himself as a person rewarded with affection and approval, with money and practical success was an impossible ideal and the sooner he accepted existing conditions the happier he would be. Yet he continued to write verse, including his "Sapphics," which pleased him a good deal, and he rearranged the collection of sonnets for his new friends, Messrs. Copeland and Day.

In the spring, "Lyrics of Earth" appeared after long delays during which the publishers accused him of keeping for a month or two, proof which was actually returned the following day. Most of the poems he had written years before. He had waited a long time to see them in print. Yet, when it was at last published, the book aroused little interest.

Today, "Lyrics of Earth" when compared with "Among the Millet" is a less interesting book but more perfect poetry. There is a narrower range of subject, but there is a higher, more even workmanship. To be sure, the sonnets of the first book, some of which had risen to heights of feeling and expression, are lacking; but so are the long narrative poems, the touches of false sentiment, the faulty or too studied versification and diction. In the main, the change was toward sobriety and simplicity. "After Rain," "Snow," and "An Autumn Landscape" are examples of a welcome condensation in landscape description and an increased intensity of feeling. The philosophy of "In May" or "Winter Store" is a little clearer and more sure, and as he stands among the mullein stalks in "In November," it is a soberer Lampman than the one who recorded his emotions in "Among the Timothy."

The publication of the book of sonnets which he believed to be the best he could produce had to be given up finally. The public taste had to be considered, and for commercial reasons the sonnet collection was split up and distributed among other poems, so that his pet plan was never realized.

It is evident that there were in him at this time strong, courageous impulses toward emotional expression, but it is equally clear that there was always lurking in the background, in these days, the sense of futility and failure, against which he made pathetic appeal in that "Invocation" which begins the sonnet section of the Collected Poems:

> "Spirit of joy and that enchanted air
> That feeds the poet's parted lips like wine,
> I dreamed and wandered hand in hand of thine,
> How many a blissful day; but doubt and care,
> The ghostly masters of this world, did come
> With torturous malady and hid the day,
> A gnawing flame that robbed my songs away,
> And bound mine ears, and made me blind and dumb.
> Master of mine, and Lord of light and ease,
> Return, return, and take me by the hand;
> Lead me again into that pleasant land,
> Whose charmèd eyes and griefless lips adore
> No lord but beauty; let me see once more
> The light upon her golden palaces.

CHAPTER XIII.

THE LAST CANOE TRIP.

URING the summer of 1896 Lampman had not been very well. He was tired with the routine and confinement of the office and looked forward with great delight to his annual three weeks' holiday. This year it had been arranged at least six months in advance, for he and his two brothers-in-law were to make a canoe trip to Lake Temagami.

At midnight they boarded the Canadian Pacific train at Ottawa for an eight-hour journey up the south bank of the Ottawa river to the Hudson's Bay depot, Mattawa. Their equipment consisted of an excellent 16-ft. birch bark canoe of Indian make; a good tent; a bag a-piece for clothing and blankets and another for cooking utensils; a large water-proof slipcase for provisions, called the "grubbix"; rifle, guns, fishing tackle, camera and a few small articles. For reading matter there were Gray's Botany, Aeschylus and the Tusculan Disputations. The classics were a provision against a rainy day in camp, and the Botany was for all weathers, as Lampman was forever botanizing. Arriving at Mattawa, in the morning they changed trains to a branch line which, crossing the Ottawa river, proceeds up its northern shore past the famous Long Sault Rapids, roaring and dashing white in the sunlight, to Kippawa, then the distributing point for the lumber camps north and east of the river. Arriving there at noon, they boarded the small steamer "Meteor," which carried supplies a hundred miles distant up the river to Lake Temiskaming. Their fellow passengers they found to consist of a celebrated English sportsman with his three Indian guides, a dear old garrulous clergyman who told of the thirty-pound lake trout he had taken, and David Maclaren, a fire-ranger of the Temagami country and one of the most famous woodsmen in Canada. By sundown the steamer had made its way up the river to where the Montreal and Metabechawan rivers join the Ottawa. Here, with considerable care, the canoe was lowered from the steamer deck into the water and the kit and men placed in it. That night they camped on the sandy beach near the mouth of the Metabechawan beside a log house, the last they would see before reaching the Hudson's Bay post at Temagami, sixty-five miles inland.

Between the Ottawa and the interior rises a bank a thousand feet high, so it was decided to get the occupant of the log house to take the kit in his wagon over this, the heaviest portage in Canada. This done, they came to a small lake, one of a series connected by the Metabechawan River; the canoe was launched and the paddling began. From this lake they passed on through rapids into another, at the end of which they encountered the Stanley Rapids, very swift and shallow. Here they were overtaken by the fire ranger who invited them to spend the night at his camp, and under whose guidance they navigated the rapids, though with great difficulty. Once the canoe grounded and all had to leap out and push the craft along, so that it was almost dark when they saw the ranger's tent glimmering ahead among the trees, large and capacious enough to hold them all. Soon a great fire was blazing in front of it and they were cooking a supper that tasted better than anything they had had for months. What an evening they spent gathered round the fire listening to the ranger's tales of adventure in the north country and joining in the French-Canadian songs of *Marlbrough s'en va-t-en guerre* or *En roulant ma boule.* How soundly they slept on their beds of balsam boughs, the wind making eternal music in the pines and bringing now and then the distant hooting of the great horned owl like a vague foreboding of disaster. The poet's ability to perpetuate the poignancy of that night is beautifully shown in the following sonnet:

NIGHT IN THE WILDERNESS

The good fire-ranger is our friend to-night;
  We sit before his tent and watch his fire
Send up its fount of sailing sparks that light
  The ruddy pine stems. Hands that never tire
Our friend's are, as he spreads his frugal store,
  And cooks his bouillon with a hunter's pride,
Till, warm with woodland fare and forest lore,
  We sink at last to sleep. On every side,
A grim mysterious presence, vast and old,
The forest stretches leagues on leagues away,
With lonely rivers running dark and cold,
  And many a gloomy lake and haunted bay.
The stars above the pines are sharp and still.
  The wind scarce moves. An owl hoots from the hill.

Next morning the ranger suggested that they go with him back into the woods to a lake which he knew was filled with beautiful trout. They started at noon, carrying the two canoes over a one-mile portage through the thick woods. The lake proved to be very beautiful, and Lampman and the ranger paddled round its shores admiring the tall trees and the rocks, thick with green moss. It was warm work, paddling under the hot northern sun and the sight of the cool, still water was too much for the poet who had always been a swimmer. So he had his swim alone. But by the time he had struggled, damp and cold, into his clothes again, the sun had gone down and the air become suddenly chill. Indeed all the party felt cold on the way back to the camp, and when they arrived, Lampman was blue and shivering. Soon they had a fire going, but he had contracted cold which caused some doubt as to the advisability of going on, and which indeed, he did not shake off during the rest of the trip, though the others spared him as much as they could.

The next day, too, was an arduous one. The first portage led over a mountain, the second was easy, the third very trying. While they were resting after this exertion, a party of Indians arrived, looking dark and sullen but good-natured and skilfull enough to hold their canoe almost motionless in the swift stream while they were being photographed. That was a marvellously beautiful spot, the river only a hundred feet wide flowing rapidly between banks at least eight hundred feet high. But it was necessary to push on, for night comes rapidly in these narrow valleys. Indeed, before they had reached the shores of Lake Makatewiguaydon darkness had overtaken them, and they had lighted their lantern and trudged on over rocks and fallen trees, the canoe packs on their shoulders. By the time supper was over it was too late to hunt up balsam boughs, so they slept—quite soundly to be sure—on the moss-covered rocks.

Next morning when they awoke a white frost covered the ground, but there lay the lake shimmering blue in the early light. The great pines grew down to the very water's edge and beyond the wooded islands scattered over its surface, rose the blue background of the mountains. That day they paddled sixteen miles through Rabbit Lake, under a clear sky, with a favouring breeze from the north. The paddling was done chiefly by Lampman's companions, for though he was an adept, his mind would often be carried away by the spell of the north country and he would sit motionless in the canoe, lost in reverie and enjoyment.

At noon they reached Rabbit Point, where their route took a sharp turn at right angles. Here they found that the name was due to the fact that a large glacial boulder there bore a striking resemblance to a sitting rabbit, and the Indians had emphasized the likeness by placing two sharp rocks for ears in a cleft back of the head and by scratching a large disc for the eye on each side. They camped that night on a rocky, moss-covered point at the end of White Bear Lake, where they were joined by a tall, sombre Indian who could speak neither English nor French, but who, after warming himself thoroughly at their fire, rolled himself in his blankets and slept without shelter on an island not far off.

Travelling on next day in company with the Indian who seemed to be going their way, they traversed several small lakes and three portages. At one of these they came upon a band of twelve Indians, men, women and children, provided with canoes, luggage and curious old shot guns with very long barrels and brass locks. The chief was a tall, erect man, the impassive expression of whose face was a relic of Indian stoicism of old. His squaw was very dark, and so old that time seemed to have forgotten her. They were on their way to their winter hunting grounds, which were allotted by mutual agreement to the various Indian families. The tepees in which they lived were made of sheets of birch bark placed upon crossed sticks, and when the travellers came upon them were helping themselves out of a steaming pot to ducks and rabbits which they ate without seasoning. It was evident that the Indians were very superstitious, for that morning the one accompanying the travellers had taken pains to paddle as far as possible from a certain island which they later learned was Snake Island, where, in a deep cleft in a rock, a snake is thought to dwell which first overcomes its victims with sleep and then kills them by its sting.

That night they reached the eastern arm of Lake Temagami, where a stiff gale was blowing up such a sea along fifteen miles of open water that they prepared to stay till it had abated. The storm lasted two days, during which there was time to rest and read and write. Of such experiences the following poem was born:

TEMAGAMI

Far in the grim Northwest beyond the lines
That turn the rivers eastward to the sea,
Set with a thousand islands, crowned with pines,
Lies the deep water, wild Temagami:
Wild for the hunter's roving, and the use
Of trappers in its dark and trackless vales,
Wild with the trampling of the giant moose,
And the weird magic of old Indian tales.
All day with steady paddles toward the west
Our heavy-laden long canoe we pressed:
All day we saw the thunder-travelled sky
Purpled with storm in many a trailing tress,
And saw at eve the broken sunset die
In crimson on the silent wilderness.

The Hudson's Bay Company's post, which is on Bear Island toward the centre of the star-shaped Lake Temagami, was reached after a six hours' stiff paddle down the northeastern arm. The weather was bitterly cold, and the heavily clouded sky cast a wan light over the grey water and the denuded island on which stood the factor's house, made of logs and plank sawn out by hand. Here the Indians received their annual bounty and in the Spring traded for supplies and ammunition for the furs which they had caught during the winter. The factor welcomed them warmly, for few white men came his way.

That night they camped close by at Metagama Point,

protected from the wind, and would have liked to stay on indefinitely. The black bass rose to the fly even in late summer and pike were easily caught with the troll. There were plenty of ducks. At night they could hear the crying of the loons, and it must have been some such moment which prompted the stanza in "The Lake in the Forest," which is addressed to Manitou, the Spirit of the Earth:

> Thy soul is in the splendour of the night,
> When silent shadows darken from the shores,
> And all the swaying fairies over floors
> Of luminous water lying strange and bright,
> Are spinning mists of silver in the moon;
> When out of magic bays
> The yells and demon laughter of the loon
> Startle the hills and raise
> The solitary echoes far away;
> Then thou art present, Spirit, wild as they.

On the return, paddling toward the end of Lake Temagami, they saw in a distant canoe three figures whom they knew by the strokes of their paddles to be white men. Fellow voyagers in the wilds are always welcome and these proved to be a professor from Yale with two students.

At the head of Rabbit Lake, which stretches out in this part for fifteen miles from north to south, they encountered a furious gale from the south-east. Soon the waves ran so high that at every pitch of the canoe the man in the prow was soaked with spray. As they were making little headway, they landed for lunch under the lea of a bluff, and one of the party, taking his gun, disappeared into the forest and in half an hour returned with a good supply of partridges. But it was necessary to find a more suitable place to camp in preparation for the rain, which they knew would soon follow. Pushing on into the centre of the lake, they found the wind stronger than ever. The canoe shipped water every time a wave struck the bow, so the only course was to work across the lake, keeping head up to the seas, for to get into the trough of the waves would have meant disaster. By dint of hard paddling they finally reached a protected cove. Rain was already falling, but soon the tent was up and there they stayed safely sheltered from the gale, which all that day and night howled riotously in the treetops over-head. Toward dawn the wind shifted and came whistling down into the door of the tent, apparently direct from the Arctic Ocean.

But all the days were not so cold, and sometimes they would paddle into a silent lake which seemed quietly dreaming of Indian summer. Once, as they were gliding across the dark surface of such a lake, they approached the bank and saw in front of them, against the background of brown water and rich foliage, a single fire-weed lighted up by a sudden shaft of light. It was such moments in the north country that stirred the heart of the poet and found expression in his verse.

One morning, on the return trip, while cooking breakfast they heard the wolves barking not more than a hundred yards from the camp. They were evidently chasing a deer which was making for the water, but did not come in sight. It is a strange sound, half bark and half bay; a sound not only of pursuit but of summoning for the rest of the pack to join in the awful chase.

With the departure of the ranger and one of the party to keep an appointment, Lampman and his companion were left to complete the journey alone. They were now going down the Metabechawan with the current and were able to run many of the rapids without mishap. At one of their camps they came upon a large colony of ravens, jet black birds, somewhat larger than the crow, which disappear upon the approach of civilization. This was a large colony, and they kept up a continual conversation with croaks that sounded almost like the bark of dogs. Lampman was always a keen observer of birds and plants. Upon arriving at a camping place, he would help put up the tent while another was making the fire and would then be likely to wander off into the woods and come back with some specimen of leaf or flower or berry. Out would come the Gray's Botany, and the search for identification begin. There would be many false starts. Finally he would announce, to the great relief of the company, that he had found it; but they would no sooner have relapsed into contentment than the discovery of some conflicting detail would set the poet on his search all over again. His friend, Professor Macoun, had once mentioned to him the existence of a rare pink northern Ontario water lily. He was always searching for that but never found it—a sort of floral Holy Grail.

Coming into Lake Temiscamingue toward the end of the trip, he there found inspiration for the following sonnet:

ON LAKE TEMISCAMINGUE

A single dreamy elm, that stands between
The sombre forest and the wan-lit lake,
Halves with its slim gray stem and pendent green
The shadowed point. Beyond it without break
Bold brows of pine-topped granite bend away,
Far to the southward, fading off in grand
Soft folds of looming purple. Cool and gray,
The point runs out, a blade of thinnest sand.
Two rivers meet beyond it; wild and clear,
Their deepening thunder breaks upon the ear—
The one descending from its forest home
By many an eddied pool and murmuring fall—
The other cloven through the mountain wall,
A race of tumbled rocks, a roar of foam.

On reaching the high portage down to the Ottawa at

the mouth of the Montreal River, they found that the continued rains had made the bank a mass of slippery clay, so following the precedent of other paddlers, they loaded everything into the canoe and carefully slid it down the bank. Half way down, they encountered in the trail a lordly skunk, who showed no sign of fear. Lampman would not have it shot, and it presently moved on, not entirely unconscious, apparently, of its standing with the men.

From here they took the steamer again to Kippawa, just above the Long Sault Rapids, which are five miles long and the most famous in Canada. Lampman had always wanted to run them, but everyone advised him not to do so. The previous year a lumberman had been drowned in the attempt when the water was much higher. They consulted an Indian, but when he had seen the canoe and the load, he refused to pilot them. An offer of five dollars, a big sum in those days, did not tempt him, so there was nothing for it but to go by train to a point below the rapids and paddle on down the river. They continued to encounter many difficult and dangerous rapids, and the procedure was to pull the canoe up and then go ahead to inspect them. Lampman always wanted to make the attempt, his companion generally had to advise caution. Usually it would end with them carrying the canoe around, though the poet invariably thought that they could have got through. He seemed not to know what physical fear was, and the only effective argument which could be used was consideration for his wife and child at home.

Reaching Mattawa, then the location of the Hudson's Bay post and two lumbermens' boarding houses, they did risk shooting the rapids there. First they crossed to the north side of the river so as to run the rapids diagonally with the main current. It was a glorious experience, the two men in the midst of the racing water and dashing spray, one guiding the boat at the stern, Lampman in the prow, his shouts scarcely audible above the roar of the waters.

After this came the prosaic train journey back to Ottawa; to the confinement, the routine, the narrower life. The poet was as tanned as an Indian. But the people at the office noticed that he did not look as well as usual. He had not spared himself. It was to be the last trip.

CHAPTER XIV.

LEAVE OF ABSENCE.

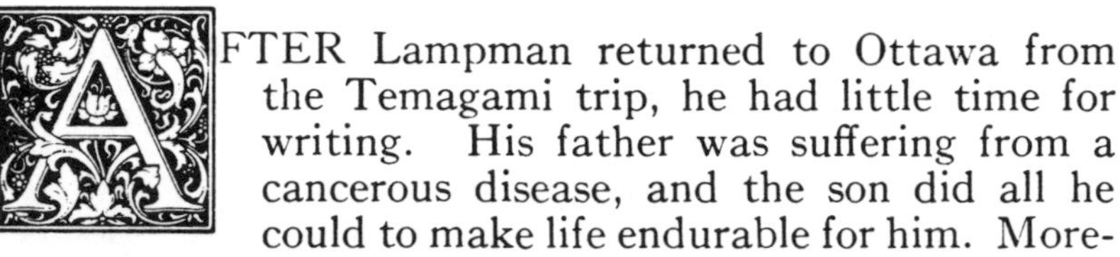

AFTER Lampman returned to Ottawa from the Temagami trip, he had little time for writing. His father was suffering from a cancerous disease, and the son did all he could to make life endurable for him. Moreover, at the office, work increased so that he had still less leisure. In the autumn he had moved into another house, 187 Bay Street, where he hoped to do some good work and indeed felt that had he had less to bother him, he would have been able to write a small book of verse in a single month. But he was growing tired of writing for the publishers. They had been too difficult to please and too dilatory in carrying out contracts. He resolved from then on to write only for himself and the few friends who understood his work and ideals. All ambition for practical success, he said, had been long since taken out of him. Yet he continued half-hearted negotiations with Messrs. Copeland and Day, who had promised to publish a new book if "Lyrics of Earth" sold well.

On March 11th, 1897, his father died after a long and painful illness, but without the suffering at the last that all had feared, and soon after Lampman rented his house and moved out to Britannia, a suburb on the Lac des Chienes. There he spent the week-ends with his wife and Natalie, and the other evenings in a little room at his father-in-law's on Sandy Hill. He had done almost no writing since his December impulse and was very much discouraged. To his friend Thomson he said that he had never been anything but a minor poet who had sometimes managed to hit upon things uncommonly near the excellent, and begged him not to over-rate his good work nor under-rate the lesser. Like every other poet he said, he had written a good deal of secondary verse. It was not prompted by the full stream of inspiration, but nevertheless he felt it not in vain, for it gave him a few hours now and then of pleasurable activity before he should be gathered in to that same ample oblivion which awaits all men.

In June, the Royal Society made a trip to Halifax to attend the Cabot celebration and Lampman, as a member, availed himself of the cheap railroad fares and the hospitality offered the Society. He had for a travelling companion, strangely enough, the same Wilfred Campbell who had formerly regarded him as an enemy. But on this occasion, save for reciting with blood-curdling fervour excerpts from his five dramas, Campbell behaved very well, and continued to impress Lampman as a man unlike himself, for whom people would do things and who would in the end be successful. At Halifax he saw Professor Tyler who had tried to get him a place at Cornell, and on the way home he stopped at Amherst for two days to visit his friend, Mr. Dickey.

Those were the days of the bicycling craze, and Lampman kept trying to sell some verses in order to buy a machine. He did buy one for his wife, but he himself continued to ride other people's, though in the process of learning he got pitched over an embankment into a patch of wild raspberry bushes. He was quite vigorous at that time, and on the same day as the bicycling accident paddled ten miles, portaging his own canoe. Poetry for a number of months was all but neglected.

His holidays that summer began on the last day of

August, and he and Duncan Campbell Scott spent them together in a ten days' trip up the Gatineau. From Maniwaki, twenty-eight miles above Ellard's, they teamed nine miles into the woods to the Joseph River. Up this small and winding stream they made their way with the canoe; sometimes wading and pushing it over sand bars, sometimes lifting it bodily over obstructions, sometimes hacking their way through with an axe. The Joseph was a beautiful little brown river broadening here and there into black pools, and the tracks of the deer were everywhere upon the open spaces along its banks. From it they portaged into Lake Achigan, a solitary sheet of brown water with the thick woods crowding in on every side, a barrier of foliage and timber which few ever penetrated. Here they camped and ate partridges and black bass, and lived so simple a life that Lampman wrote reckless verses, "An Invitation to the Woods," which he called doggerel, but which were bought by the "Youth's Companion" for $25, much to his amazement.

"Lyrics of Earth" had not sold well, and Messrs. Copeland Day, having decided to publish no further Lampman works at present, he resolved to print his own through a British firm. He estimated that he could sell enough copies in six months to pay for publication and have any additional sales for himself, beside being able to rid himself of obligation to publishers.

Some years before this his poetry had attracted the notice of another writer, chiefly of prose tales of pioneer days, Hamlin Garland, and a correspondence had sprung up between the two men. Late in 1897 Garland, who needed a holiday and who was anxious to collect facts about the Klondyke, planned a trip to Canada and arranged to visit Lampman in Ottawa. Visits from kindred spirits from across the border were rare, and the two men had some interesting walks and talks together and at least one standing joke in the family arose from the fact that the bed provided for the guest was so short that the Westerner had some difficulty in adjusting himself to its limitations. Lampman found him a fine, genial-minded, good-humoured American soul, a little distraught and careworn as if from over-work, and Garland saw in his host more than ever a man devoted to the finer things of life.

All this time Lampman had himself been suffering, not so much from over-work as over-exertion. It is probable that his childhood affliction left his heart weakened, and this was increased by violent exercise and particularly by the cold and labour experienced on his last camping trip in Temagami. In the winter of 1897 he began to notice that vigorous exercise caused him pain and exhaustion, and by the following winter he could not walk a hundred feet without having to stop until the pain had subsided. The doctor immediately ordered him to bed, where he remained for a month, and it was another month before he could leave his room. When April came, he was able to get out of doors and crawl about like an old man of ninety, he said, to whom a stair is a serious bugbear. In appearance he was much as usual, but he suffered intense pain at any extra exertion, since his heart had to keep up normal circulation and at the same time overcome the deficiency caused by the weakening and thickening of the mitral valve. The only remedy was total inactivity, both physical and mental. Thus he had to content himself with a little reading, mostly history and memoirs, and with dreams of a cottage in some sunlit rolling country where, a pensioner of the government, he might cultivate a small garden and write verse to his heart's content.

In January the Department had granted him a three months' leave of absence, which was extended into six months' leave. By the end of May he was beginning to plan for the trip which the doctor said was possible and necessary. On June 21st, 1898, his third child, Archibald Otto, was born. Finally, when his family affairs had been arranged and funds had been provided by his friends, he was able to leave for Montreal.

He had not often left Ottawa, but he had, in Montreal, nevertheless, warm friends in fellow writers like William Henry Drummond, Arthur Stringer, W. D. Lighthall and William McLennan.

One of these friends, Arthur Stringer, then in newspaper work, has left a record of a visit paid, one night, to Lampman when he was Drummond's guest. Arriving at the Drummond house, Stringer was ushered upstairs to a rear second-story porch. Hot darkness hung over the city. The only light was from the moon and the street lamps filtering through the motionless maple leaves and from the cigarettes of the smokers on the porch. Drummond rose to greet his guest. "As the light came on," says Stringer, "the second man rose to his feet. He had been squatting on the floor, boy-like, with a couple of sofa pillows under him, his hands linked tranquilly over his knee, his face turned toward the river bend beyond the heated city crowned with its luminous haze of dust. This second figure was Archibald Lampman, the purest poet, the greatest apostle of beauty who ever drew the breath of life within the Dominion of Canada. I peered at him and thought of Browning's line: 'And so you once saw Shelley plain'." In Lampman, he saw a similarity to Shelley and Shakespeare and Raphael in what he called "the effeminacy of genius." The meaning of the term is not altogether clear, but the statement is true if by it he meant that innate refinement, and purity, and devotion to ideals always associated with the highest type of womanhood. They talked that night about many and varied subjects, so that it was late when Stringer's visit terminated. "From it," he says, "I carried away one indelible impression, and that impression was that beside me had sat a man who did not wear his spirit of poetry as an exquisite wears a rose-bud, but one who lived in and for the quest of beauty, as men live and die in the mere quest of bread, of gold, of the material and sordid play-things of the world. He did not carry the torch it seemed to me: he was the torch itself."

On this occasion Lampman was also a guest at 913 Dorchester Street, where a group of bachelors extended to him a convivial hospitality. Andrew McPhail had been one of their number; E. W. Thomson was a welcome guest; of those living there at the time, David Walker was interested in theatre enterprises, Richard Lee was an inestimable *raconteur* and Edmond Dyonnet, a local painter. Lampman's host was Dr. Tait McKenzie, who later became head of physical training in the University of Pennsylvania and a sculptor with an international reputation. They had met in 1895, when the Doctor was on the staff at Government House, Ottawa, and the occasion was a Vice-Regal garden party. McKenzie had been struck by Lampman's air of quiet aloofness from his surroundings; a conversation had begun, and they had spent the rest of the evening in considerable neglect of their obligations to Ottawa society.

Into the carefree, masculine life of the Dorchester Street house Lampman entered with a great deal of enjoyment. He laughed at Lee's jokes, posed for Dyonnet's pictures, and even tried to make out-door sketches himself, expressing great satisfaction at being able to draw sheep distinguishable from rocks. The bachelors and their friends did much to make him forget his sickness and depression.

Drummond was a member of the St. Maurice Club,

which had a lodge in the Lake Wayagamack country, and after a time it was arranged for Lampman to go there as a guest. He journeyed by train to Three Rivers and by weekly steamer, seventy miles, to La Tuque; then by canoe or road seven miles to the comfortable club house built of logs. The life there suited him entirely. The fishing was good; the air was like elixir; the caretaker and his wife looked after all his wants. But by the first of September he had to be on his way, as he had planned to visit Digby and Boston before his leave expired. Yet he commemorated his vist to the wilds in the following sonnet:

WAYAGAMACK

Beautiful are thy hills, Wayagamack,
Thy depths of lonely rock, thine endless piles
Of grim birch forest and thy spruce-dark isles,
Thy waters fathomless and pure and black,
But golden where the gravel meets the sun,
And beautiful thy twilight solitude,
The gloom that gathers over lake and wood
A weirder silence when the day is done
For ever wild, too savage for the plough,
Thine austere beauty thou canst never lose.
Change shall not mar thy loneliness, nor tide
Of human trespass trouble thy repose,
The Indian's paddle and the hunter's stride
Shall jar thy dream and break thy peace enow.

At Quebec, he stopped to see Canon Frederick George Scott and to explore the town, which he found very attractive with its "corners and alleyways where there are ancient buildings, remnants of walls, fortifications, etc., intensely interesting and picturesque." "You must," he wrote to McKenzie, "come to Quebec for masterpieces of nature and age." Of the journey to St. John and Digby he wrote to the same friend:

"My journey down here was satisfactory all through, but the little bit from St. John to Digby by steamer was immense. St. John harbour was full of haze and thin fog—flooded with silver sunshine of the early morning, and all the masts and chimneys, smoke-stacks, roofs and old chocolate-coloured wharfs at low tide were dim and spectral through a misty glory. I had never seen anything like this before. It was gorgeous."

He stayed in Digby till the end of September, visiting his relatives, descendants of Nova Scotia Gesners, whom he had not met before. The sea air and the unusual surroundings suited his mood, and the people must have appealed to his pictorial sense for he wrote to McKenzie as follows:

"Yesterday I hired a little sea-dog with curly iron-grey hair, swarthy, ruddy complexion, blue eyes, in dark red jersey, navy blue trousers and greyish white hat, and we tacked about in his sail-boat all afternoon in a fine breeze—good fun. He is going to take me next week for some deep sea fishing—haddock and codfish."

Of Digby itself he wrote:

"This is a very picturesque town, and here are some delightfully quiet little old gardens full of flowers and fruit and things mixed up together, gnarly quince trees and ancient cherries—pleasant places for an hour's dreaming."

Doubtless the pleasantest part of the trip was the few October days spent with his friend Thomson in Boston. He used to say that Boston made him feel another man intellectually, and that when he returned to Ottawa he seemed gradually to freeze up. Yet his eager family, on his return, found him improved in health, and although the office seemed to him a very Saharah of Official Dreariness, October 15th found him back again at work.

That winter he lived in a very careful and abstemious fashion and interested himself agreeably in the proofs of a new book, "Alcyone," which the Constables of Edinburgh were to bring out. Every day he continued to read a little Greek, a page or two before breakfast, and said dryly that he found it a great deal easier than he found Browning. Looking back on his life, it seemed to him that he had mismanaged it abominably. He wished for two things: that he might have seen more of life when he was in his twenties and that throughout he might have had the counsel of some good and wise man. He tried to write, but could not. He was less morbid than he had been. He was living in a sort of grey calm, but it was really a calm, not the turmoil of discontent, and he thought that with a return of bodily activity his Muse would waken again.

Toward the end of January, 1899, he had an attack of *la grippe*, which kept him away from the office for a few days, but he was back again by Wednesday, February 8th. It was a cold day in the middle of the Canadian winter, but after work at the office he went for a long walk. Next morning he was unable to get up, and the doctor, when summoned, said that he was suffering from an attack of acute pneumonia. All that day his wife tended him carefully. He was suffering considerably, but was not unduly alarmed. Pain and lassitude were too familiar for that. As darkness came on his condition grew worse. It was a typical Canadian winter night. The weather was cold, but there was little wind, and the snow fell silently upon the towers of Parliament Hill, the broad reaches of frozen river and the little house at the corner of Bay and Slater streets. There, when the city clocks were faintly striking the hour of one in the morning, Archibald Lampman died.

The first accounts of Lampman's death and his burial in Beechwood Cemetery were perfunctory and hastily written in the Canadian press. But several days later editorials and selections from his poems were published by various papers. By one he was called "Canada's long-accepted foremost exponent of the Beautiful, to read whose poetry was to enter an atmosphere so calm and undismayed that one girded up one's loins for the battle of living with renewed strength." "Nothing in nature as we know it," said another, "can ever again seem commonplace, for he felt the inspiration and revealed its worth. He was a poet of Canada, and the Canada which mourns his death is a richer and better land because of what he did and what he was." His home paper, the "Ottawa Evening Journal," wrote of him with such sympathy that his mother said that she had not thought that anyone could have understood her son so well. It spoke of the busy life of a new country where "the voice of the singer is scarcely heard amid the roar of steam whistle, the grunt of engine or clang of hammers, the clatter of business and the buzz of politics," and concluded: . . . "While we need not blame ourselves, each pioneer of us in this new encampment being pressed by his own tasks, we may be permitted to wish that Archibald Lampman had been more favoured by fate in his personal and literary environment. While he was with us he was accepted as a matter of course, as living men are; but it will be strange if his name is forgotten or his work unread or unvalued as time goes on."

Equally sympathetic were the contemporary poets for many of whom Lampman's death was a personal loss. This was particularly true of Duncan Campbell Scott, who had been for years his closest friend. Wilfred Campbell's "Bereavement of the Fields," a lament for Lampman, is one of his best and sincerest poems, and was printed at the beginning of Lampman's Collected Poems, edited with a memoir by Dr. Scott and published through the kindness of friends, particularly George Iles, and with the assistance of the Canadian press. Memorial verses were written by a number of Canadian poets; Jean Blewett, Lally Bernard, Charles G. Rogers, Mary Hasbrouck and Lyman Smith, the conclusion of whose sonnet read:

> Though dear the loss of that unfinished strain
> Though skilful hand and tuneful lip be gone,
> He hath not swept the string nor sung in vain.
> The song that swelled with hope and loving trust
> Shall e'er in cheerful notes go ringing on,
> Nor die and be enshrouded with his dust.

That this hope has been fulfilled is evident from the regard which Canadians have had for Lampman ever since. Now that more than a quarter of a century has elapsed since his death, it is possible to estimate his work without bias. It is apparent that since he was not a pioneer and did not identify himself with movements, such as Whitman's, which have influenced modern American verse, he remains largely a product of his period. Since then, styles have changed and some of his verse has become out-moded. Moreover, even in his own time his choice of subject was not invariably happy, his narratives were not always of consequence, and his Utopian philosophy was sometimes too vaguely optimistic. Nor did he escape charges of repetition, prolixity and over-studied writing. Of the five hundred pages of Lampman poems which exist perhaps only one-fifth is of high merit, but that displays qualities of insight and beauty, sweetness and power and imagination which continue a credit to him and to the country and period in which it was produced.

The choice of these best poems will depend upon the varying tastes of readers who will seek in them descriptions of scenery, nature, philospohy, emotional release, biographical comment, or stylistic perfection. By virtue of an old philosophy expressed under new conditions, "Heat" and "The Frogs" are almost famous. Others are "Winter Hues Recalled," with its Wordsworthian view of the sustaining power of recollection; "The Comfort of the Fields," its Nature, beautiful in aspect as well as thought; "The Return of the Year," pulsing with passion for the Spring; "After Rain," a beautiful balance of the pictorial and emotional; the "Ode to the Hills," so noble in conception and expression; and "The Lake in the Forest," probably the highest achievement in Canadian forest verse thus far. As examples of his varied skill in style there is the exquisite lyricism of "Before Sleep," the originality of "By an Autumn Stream," and "Personality," the careful artistry of the sonnets. That these were considered his finest work both by himself and others is because he was best in the short flights and the compact form which they necessitated. Of them, "Beauty" and "Uplifting" are thoughtful; "Late November," "April Night," and "A Sunset at Les Eboulements" pictorial; "Sirius," impassioned; "In Absence," simple and sincere; and "Music,"[1] of a spiritual exaltation welcome in any literature. His less popular narrative verse is not negligible, for "The Violinist" and the "Vase of Ibn Mokbil" are good poetry and "Alcyone" better, and in spite of undue Tennysonian influence and a lack of reality there is much merit in "The Story of an Affinity" as well as in certain moments in "An Athenian Reverie" and "David and Abigail."

In retrospect, his brief, uneventful life goes by as in a series of pictures—the Nature-haunted schoolboy, the studious youth, the developing college man, the unhappy teacher, the plodding postoffice clerk. He was, too, a devoted son and husband, a tender father and a staunch

[1] "O, take the lute this brooding hour for me."

friend. Above all, he was an earnest poet; at times fired with inspiration, at others cold in despondency. He was all these, but never the coward. He longed to be free, but was hemmed in by work and poverty; he wished to be vigorous, but was prevented by ill-health; he yearned for recognition which did not come. Yet Archibald Lampman was not a martyr. Fate did not deal more harshly with him than with other men, but he was more sensitive than most men, and perhaps more conscious than most, of the goal of perfection toward which he must strive. It is that steadfast devotion to the ideal which was his finest characteristic. That is the inspiring force which gives wings to his verse. It is that which beautifies and reanimates his life.

THE END

APPENDIX

AND

INDEX

APPENDIX

BIBLIOGRAPHY

LAMPMAN POEMS IN MAGAZINES

Atlantic Monthly

- Jan., 1891. Snowbirds.
- Feb., 1892. With the Night.
- March, 1894. City of the End of Things.
- Jan., 1895. Alcyone.
- March, 1899. The Largest Life.

Canadian Magazine

- Oct., 1896. Chione.
- Nov., 1903. Indian Summer.
- Jan., 1914. New Year's Eve.
- Dec., 1913. Settler's Tale.

Century

- May, 1885. Bird Voices.
- Sept., 1893. Storm Voices.
- July, 1895. The Passing of the Spirit.

The Chap-Book

- Jan. 15, 1895. Inter Vias.
- Nov. 1, 1895. Wind and World.

Cosmopolitan

- Nov., 1891. A Midnight Landscape.
- Jan., 1892. A March Day.
- Feb., 1893. After Mist in Winter.
- June, 1893. June. (Ill. by Hamilton Gibson).
- March, 1895. Personality. War. (Painting by Pierre Fritel).

The Current

- Jan. 17, 1885. A January Sunset.

Current Literature

- Feb., 1900. The Largest Life.

Harper's

- Feb., 1890. The Sun Cup.
- Nov., 1890. In November.
- Jan., 1891. March of Winter.
- June, 1892. Sleep.
- Oct., 1892. An Autumn Landscape.
- Sept., 1893. September
- Aug., 1896. Song of Pan.
- Sept., 1898. Uplifting.

Independent

- May 22, 1890. River Dawn. (A Dawn on the Lièvre).
- Aug. 14, 1890. Across the Pea Fields.
- Mar. 5, 1891. In March.
- Mar. 5, 1891. Winter Break.
- Apr. 9, 1891. The Meadow.
- Oct. 1, 1891. A Sunset on the Lower St. Lawrence. (Les Eboulements).

Dec. 3, 1891. SUNSET.
Aug. 25, 1892. AT THE FERRY.
1892. THE POET'S SONG.
Mar. 2, 1893. CLOUD-BREAK.
Apr. 13, 1893. BEFORE THE ROBIN.
Apr. 5, 1894. SUCCESSORS OF PAN. (Favourites of Pan)
July 26, 1894. THE WIND'S WORD.
Mar. 9, 1899. THE VIOLINIST.
Aug. 31, 1899. VASE OF IBN MOKBIL.

Lippincott's

Sept., 1914. UNREST.

Living Age

Jan. 31, 1903. AMONG THE MILLET.
Mar. 14. 1903. OUTLOOK.

Scribner's

Sept., 1887. THE LOONS.
Nov., 1887. AN OLD LESSON FROM THE FIELDS.
June, 1888. DESPONDENCY.
Aug., 1888. MIDSUMMER NIGHT.
Dec., 1888. WINTER EVENING. (Ill. by J. H. Twachtman).
April, 1889. APRIL NIGHT.
Sept., 1889. DROUGHT.
Dec., 1889. EVENING. (Ill. by A. Lemaire).
Feb., 1890. THE MOON-PATH.
May, 1890. DEAD CITIES.
July, 1890. TO THE CRICKET.
Nov., 1890. LIFE AND NATURE.
Apr. 1891. NIGHT.
Aug., 1891. IN ABSENCE.
Oct., 1891. THE VOICES OF EARTH.
Feb., 1892. COMFORT OF THE FIELDS.
June, 1892. THE RETURN OF THE YEAR.
Nov., 1893. INDIAN SUMMER.
Dec., 1894. THE WOODCUTTER'S HUT.
Nov., 1895. THE RUIN OF THE YEAR.
May, 1897. A MAY SONG. (In May).
July, 1897. WHITE PANSIES.
Oct., 1897. WE TOO SHALL SLEEP.
Nov., 1898. THE PASSING OF AUTUMN.
March, 1899. THE WINTER STARS.

The Week

Vol. 1. A MONITION.
(1883) THREE FLOWER PETALS.
A FANTASY.
BALLADE OF SUMMER'S SLEEP.
Vol. 2. KING'S BIRTHDAY.
THE WEAVER.
Vol. 3. THE ORGANIST.
Vol. 4. ABDU MIDJAN.
THE LITTLE HANDMAIDEN.
Vol. 5. THE RAILWAY STATION.
NEW YEAR'S EVE.
WINTER.
Vol. 7. AMONG THE ORCHARDS.
Vol. 9. THE BETTER DAY.
THE CITY.
Vol. 12. A SHEAF OF SONNETS.
Virtue, Modern Politician, Ultra Protestant, Millionaire, Avarice, Stoic and Hedonist, Salvation, Cup of Life, Chaucer, Beauty.
Vol. 13. GO LITTLE BOOK.

Youth's Companion

Nov. 5, 1891. A REASSURANCE.
Dec. 3, 1891. SWEETNESS OF LIFE.

Mar. 31, 1892. GOD SPEED TO THE SNOW.
June 9, 1892. THE POET'S POSSESSION.
July 28, 1892. GOLDENROD.
Aug. 11, 1892. BY THE SEA.
Dec. 1, 1892. NATURE LOVE (On the Companionship with Nature).
Dec. 15, 1892. BESIDE THE STREAM (By an Autumn Stream).
Apr. 13, 1893. APRIL IN THE HILLS.
May 25, 1893. GOOD SPEECH.
June 22, 1893. TO THE WARBLING VIREO.
July 20, 1893. THE ANGEL OF THE HOUSE (The Spirit of the House).
Oct. 12, 1893. AFTER THE SHOWER.
May 17, 1894. TO MY DAUHGTER.
Apr. 4, 1895. DISTANCE.
May 2, 1895. MAY.
May 16, 1895. WHEN THE BOBOLINK COMES (Nesting Time).
July 25, 1895. THE CLOUD FLEET (O'er the blue beaming ocean).
Oct. 31, 1895. MYSTERY OF A YEAR.
Nov. 14, 1895. PATERNITY.
Oct. 22, 1896. NIGHT AND SLEEP (A Summer Evening).
July 22, 1897. KING OSWALD'S FEAST.
Feb. 9, 1898. YARROW.
June 23, 1898. AN INVITATION TO THE WOODS.
Feb. 9, 1899. TO THE ROBIN (Stout little preacher, houseless and unfed).
Apr. 6, 1899. HEPATICAS.

BOOKS AND PAMPHLETS

[illegible] RECORD OF THE LAMPMAN FAMILY IN CANADA. Compiled by E. Voorhis. Ottawa 1920.
TRANSACTIONS OF THE ROYAL SOCIETY OF CANADA. Sec. 2, 1921. Memories of the Poet. E. Voorhis.
GESNER FAMILY OF NEW YORK AND NOVA SCOTIA. A. T. Gesner, Middletown, Conn., 1912.
KENT HISTORICAL SOCIETY PAPERS AND ADDRESSES. Vol. 6. 1924.
PIONEERS OF OLD ONTARIO. W. L. Smith. Toronto, 1923.
CELEBRATED CANADIANS. H. J. Morgan. Quebec, 1862.
CANADIAN MEN AND WOMEN OF THE TIME. H. J. Morgan. Toronto, 1912.
LIFE AND TIMES OF THE RT. HON. SIR JOHN A. MACDONALD. J. E. Collins. Toronto, 1883.
CANADA UNDER THE ADMINISTRATION OF LORD LORNE. J. E. Collins. Toronto, 1884.
PEARLS AND PEBBLES, OR NOTES OF AN OLD NATURALIST. Catharine Parr Traill. Toronto 1895.
TRINITY COLLEGE SCHOOL RECORD. Jubilee Number. May, 1915.
ROUGE ET NOIR, AND REVIEW. Trinity College. Toronto, 1880-90.
LETTERS OF ROBERT LOUIS STEVENSON. Sidney Colvin. New York, 1911.
LETTERS OF MATTHEW ARNOLD. G. W. E. Russell. New York. London. 1900.
CAMBRIDGE HISTORY OF ENGLISH LITERATURE. Cambridge, 1918.
HISTORY OF ENGLISH-CANADIAN LITERATURE TO THE CONFEDERATION. Ray Palmer Baker. Cambridge, Mass., 1920.
REMINISCENCES, POLITICAL AND PERSONAL. Sir John Willison. Toronto, 1919.
MY WINDOWS ON THE STREET OF THE WORLD. James Mavor. London, 1913.
CANADIAN PORTRAITS. Adrian Macdonald. Toronto, 1924.
HIGHWAYS OF CANADIAN LITERATURE. J. D. Logan. Toronto, 1924.
HEADWATERS OF CANADIAN LITERATURE. Archibald MacMechan. Toronto, 1924.
AMERICAN AUTHORSHIP OF THE PRESENT DAY. T. E. Rankin. Ann Arbor, 1918.
SOCIALISM. O. D. Skelton. Boston. New York. 1911.
BLISS CARMAN. Doctoral Dissertation. H. D. Lee. Buxton, 1912.
CHARLES G. D. ROBERTS. James Cappon. Toronto, 1923.
UNPUBLISHED ESSAYS by Archibald Lampman on Keats and the Pre-Raphaelite School.
UNPUBLISHED LETTERS of Lampman to J. A. Ritchie, Ottawa; E. W. Thomson, Boston; Dr. Tait McKenzie, Montreal; W. D. Lighthall, Montreal, and Hamlin Garland, New York.

PERIODICALS.

Book Buyer. Sketch with portrait. April, 1899.

Bookman. Sketch. W. L. Wendell. August, 1900.
Canadian Poetry. P. Edgar. July, 1919.

Canadian Bookman. Canadiana. R. F. Dixon. July, 1920.

Canadian Magazine.
Canadian Poetry. Gordon Waldron. December, 1896.
Lampman Criticism. Arthur Stringer. April, 1894.
Decade of Canadian Poetry. June, 1901.
In Memory of Lampman. Lally Bernard. February, 1902.
Lampman's Birthplace. December, 1906.
Literary Group of '61. J. D. Logan. 1911.
Little talk about Lampman. E. R. Macdonald. April, 1919.
Poetry and Progress. D. C. Scott. January, 1923.
Canadian Club Year Book. Speech by B. K. Sandwell. 1919-20.
Critic. "Lyrics of Earth." Review. January 16, 1887.
Current Literature. Sketch. March, 1897.
Globe. Toronto. Article by Augusta Doan Richardson. February 18, 1889.
Harper's Magazine. Appreciation by W. D. Howells. April, 1889.
Literature. Appreciation by W. D. Howells. March, 1917.
London Academy. Review. November 23, 1889.
London Spectator. Review. January 12, 1889.
Montreal Witness. February 24, 1884, and February 10, 1889.
Munsey's Magazine. Canadian Poets. May, 1895.
North American Notes and Queries. Archibald Lampman L. J. Burpee. September, 1900.
Poet Lore. Archibald Lampman and the Sonnet. L. Untermeyer. November, 1909.
Public Opinion. Appreciation. March, 1899.
Queen's Quarterly. John Marshall, July, 1901, and Bernard Muddiman. January to March, 1915.
T. P.'s Weekly. Canadian Poets. B. Muddiman. April 16, 1909.
Transcript, Boston. Canada's Tribute to her poet. E. W. Thomson. March 14, 1914.
United Empire. Canadian Writers. A. Clyne. June, 1920.
University Magazine. Poetry of Lampman. G. H. Unwin. February, 1917.

BOOKS OF POEMS.

AMONG THE MILLET, Ottawa. J. Durie and Son, 1888.
LYRICS OF EARTH, Boston. Copeland and Day, 1895.
ALCYONE, Ottawa. James Ogilvy, 1899 (12 copies).
POEMS: Memorial Edition with Memoir. Toronto. Morang and Co. 1900.
Holiday Edition of above in two vols., 1901.
LYRICS OF EARTH; With Introduction. Toronto. Musson Book Co. 1925.

LAMPMAN IN "ROUGE ET NOIR" AND THE "REVIEW"

Dec., 1880. SHELLEY'S "REVOLT OF ISLAM." Prose.
Feb., 1881. FRIENDSHIP. Prose.
March, 1882. GERMAN PATRIOTIC POETRY. Prose.
Nov., 1882. COLLEGE DAYS AMONG OURSELVES. Prose.
Nov., 1882. THE LAST SORTIE.*
Dec., 1882. DERELICT.*
July, 1883. GAMBETTA. Prose.
May, 1884. SPRING ON THE RIVER ("O sun shine hot on the river").
March, 1885. A JANUARY SUNSET ("Again the sharp night cometh, and again").
May, 1885. THE HEPATICA* ("What faint sweet song out of the turning years").
June, 1885. AN AUGUST WARNING* ("O bleak cold wind, why must thou weep and moan").
May, 1885. BIRD VOICES ("The robin and sparrow a-wing"). From the *Century*.
Dec., 1885. AN OCTOBER SUNSET ("One moment the slim cloud flakes seem to lean"). From "Man", edited by Dr. Playter.
Dec., 1885. WINTER'S NAP* ("For a moment in the north").
Feb., 1886. HANS FINGERHUT'S FROG-LESSON (prose), from "Man" (A Fairy Tale").
July, 1886. THE THREE PILGRIMS ("In the days when the fruit of men's labour was sparing").
Nov., 1887. AN OLD LESSON FROM THE HILLS ("Even as watched the daylight how it sped"). Sonnet from *Scribner's*.
Feb., 1888. GENTLEMEN* ("Ah brothers sweet of thought so rare to find"). Sonnet.
Feb., 1888. HOPE AND FEAR* ("As when the sunless face of winter fills").
April, 1888. A GOD-SPEED TO THE SNOW ("March is slain. The keen winds fly").
May, 1890. A MORNING SUMMONS ("Upon the outer verge of sleep"). Sonnet.
Dec., 1890. GOLDENROD ("Ere the stout year be waxen shrewd and old"). Sonnet.

*Not in the COLLECTED POEMS.

INDEX